Escape AI Disruption

How to Rebuild Your Career, Business, and Learning Before AI Makes Your Old Skills Obsolete

Dedicated to my mother and Guru

Contents

Preface 5

Why AI Disruption Is Different This Time 8

Why AI Is Not Just Another Technology Trend 9

Why Smart People Still Get Disrupted 16

Why a Fixed Plan Fails and an Agile Mindset Wins 21

Why AI Will Not Replace Everyone Equally 27

What Exactly Is AI Disruption? 33

Mapping the Boundary Between Human and Machine 34

What AI Can Already Do Better, Faster, or Cheaper 40

What Skills Are Becoming Less Valuable 45

What Skills Are Becoming More Valuable 49

What Makes a Person AI-Resilient 54

When Will AI Disruption Hit You? 59

The Honest Timeline of Disruption 60

Early Warning Signals in Your Career 68

When to Pivot, Upgrade, or Reinvent 75

Where AI Disruption Will Hit First 83

Disruption by Function 84

Disruption by Industry 91

Where New Opportunities Will Be Created 98

How AI Actually Disrupts Careers and Businesses 107

The Five Levels of AI Disruption 108

How Your Job Gets Unbundled 114

How Businesses Will Use AI to Reduce Cost 120

How Learning Itself Is Changing 126

How to Escape: The Agile Reinvention Loop 131

Run Your Career Like an Agile Team 132

Step One: Audit Your Current Work 137

Step Two: Build Your AI Advantage Stack 141
Step Three: Think in Systems, Not Tasks 145
Step Four: Make Your Value Visible 149
Step Five: Visualize Your Progress 153
Step Six: Build Career Optionality 157

How Much AI Disruption Costs, and How Much to Invest 161
The Cost of Doing Nothing 162
How Much Time Should You Invest? 167
How Much Money Should You Invest? 173
How to Measure Return on Reinvention 178

The 90-Day AI Disruption Escape Roadmap 185
Set Up Your Board (Day 0) 186
Days 1-15: Awareness and Exposure Mapping 191
Days 16-30: AI Fluency Sprint 196
Days 31-60: Value Creation Sprint 201
Days 61-90: Reinvention Sprint 205

What Comes After Escaping AI Disruption? 210
From AI Survival to AI Leadership 211
The Human Advantage in an AI World 217
Reinvention Never Ends 223
You Do Not Escape AI by Running From It 229

Appendices 232
AI Disruption Self-Assessment 233
The Human-AI Boundary Map (Worksheet) 235
The Framework Toolkit: One-Page Reference Card 237
30-Day AI Learning Tracker 239
Career Risk Mapping Template 241
Human-AI Workflow Canvas 243
The Personal Reinvention Board (Kanban Template) 245
Systems Map Worksheet: Find Your Leverage Points 247
Personal Retro and Sprint Template 249
Personal Reinvention Scorecard 250

AI Tools Starter List 251
90-Day Escape Plan Workbook 253

Preface

Not long ago, a senior leader told me, with complete conviction, that a process in her organization simply could not be changed. It was, she explained, how things had been done for years. As she spoke, I kept thinking about everything outside her window that had already changed: her customers, her teams, and the way AI was reshaping workflows across her industry. Her decisions, though, ran on a playbook written more than a decade earlier. It was, to borrow an image I have used before, a bullock-cart thought process in an electric-car world.

I have seen versions of that conversation many times, and it is a large part of why this book exists.

After years of working alongside organizations through one transformation after another, I am convinced that the hardest part of any change is almost never the strategy or the tools. It is the people, and how hard it is for them to unlearn what they know, to adapt, and to feel safe while doing both. Many of those transformations failed, and rarely because the plan was wrong; they failed because we underestimated how hard the human part is. AI makes that part harder than anything I have seen before, because this time people are not only changing how they work. They are quietly questioning their own relevance.

That fear is rarely spoken aloud. In meeting after meeting, beneath the announcements and the budgets, I have felt the same unspoken tension in the room. Will AI replace me? Am I already behind? Is it safer to experiment, or to stay quiet? No one says it, yet almost everyone feels it. And so AI disruption, which nearly everyone treats as a technology problem, turns out to be a deeply human one. It cannot be forced from the top: where people do not feel safe, curiosity and experimentation disappear, and AI becomes just another costly initiative.

Watching how individuals and organizations respond, I keep seeing the same two mistakes. The first is to chase AI as a trend rather than a tool: to adopt it because a competitor announced it, a board asked about it, or a demo looked impressive, with no real problem for it to solve. Used that way, AI is an expensive decoration, a Ferrari bought for a road full of traffic. The second mistake runs in the opposite direction. It is to hand over too much, to let the tools do the thinking, and to trust outputs that are confident, polished, and almost right. And almost right, I have learned the hard way, is the most dangerous kind of wrong.

The thread running through this book is a simple correction to both. AI is a vehicle, not a destination. It enables real outcomes, not applause, and delivers the most when a capable human stays in the loop: questioning its assumptions, adding lived experience, replacing easy certainty with judgment, and deciding what is better left unsaid. The skill that matters now is not prompting a machine. It is editing, validating, and humanizing what the machine produces, because that is where trust, credibility, and leadership still live.

None of this is a reason to be afraid. Being scared that AI will take our work is, as I once put it, a way of dying a little each day, and fear adds no value to anyone. The more useful question, the one this book is built around, is what value a person can add on top of what AI already does. Look at what the machines cannot do; that is where the opportunity lies.

This book is my attempt to turn that question into a method. It does not trade in hype or in doom, but offers a practical way through. The early parts take up the plain questions of why, what, when, and where. The later parts turn to the how: a repeatable loop for reinventing how a person works, an honest sense of the time and money it takes, and a ninety-day plan concrete enough to begin on a Monday.

I have written it for the individual professional more than for the strategist, because in the end it is individuals who must learn, adapt, and stay relevant, whatever their organizations decide. The fundamentals it rests on are not new, and will outlast whatever tool is current when this is read: set a goal, iterate, reflect honestly, take in feedback, and improve daily. What is new is only the speed, and the stakes.

A last word of perspective. For all the noise, we are still early. AI has a long runway ahead of it, and these are its opening chapters, not its closing ones. The platforms being built now will create opportunities no one can yet name, much as the smartphone made room for companies that could not exist before it. Those opportunities will belong to the people who keep experimenting, who use these tools without surrendering their own judgment, and who refuse to meet a changing world with yesterday's assumptions.

That, in the end, is the argument of everything that follows, and it is worth saying plainly before the first chapter begins: you do not escape AI by running from it. You escape by learning to lead it. That is what it means to escape AI disruption, and what the pages ahead make possible.

Escape AI Disruption

PART ONE

WHY

Why AI Disruption Is Different This Time

No one escapes disruption without first understanding why this wave is unlike the ones already survived.

CHAPTER ONE

Why AI Is Not Just Another Technology Trend

Every few years, something arrives that is going to change everything. The internet. The smartphone. The cloud. Anyone who has worked for more than a decade has earned a useful skepticism about all of it, having watched "transformations" turn out to be software upgrades with a marketing budget. So when the same voice insists that artificial intelligence will change everything, folding one's arms and waiting is a fair response. This time, the waiting carries a cost, not because the hype is finally true, but because AI is a different kind of thing than the technologies that taught a generation to be skeptical.

The difference is worth stating plainly before the rest of the argument can land. Earlier waves of technology changed how the work got done. This wave changes what the work is. That is a larger claim, and the pages that follow are about why it holds, and why the usual, sensible response of waiting to see is, this once, the expensive one.

And the pace is the part that breaks intuition. Earlier tools improved on the timescale of decades, and a spreadsheet in 1990 was not radically better than one five years before. These systems improve on the timescale of months, and each improvement is cumulative and distributed to everyone at once. A skill that looks safe today is being measured against a version of the technology that will not exist by the time a person finishes reading about it. Waiting to see, the sensible default for every previous wave, quietly stops being sensible when the thing being watched grows more capable while it is being watched.

None of this means the skeptic was wrong before. Most "revolutionary" technologies really were oversold, and the habit of discounting them was earned honestly. The argument here is narrower, and therefore harder to wave away: this particular technology reaches the cognitive core of knowledge work, improves continuously, and costs almost nothing to deploy. A person can believe that most technology hype is noise and still need to take this one seriously, because the reason to take it seriously is not the volume of the hype but the specific thing the tool now does.

The Difference Between a Tool and a Colleague

The technologies of the past were tools, and a tool is an extension of the hands and the memory. A spreadsheet never decided what the numbers meant; a person did. It automated the calculating, the muscle of knowledge work, and left the thinking to the human. The thinking was the part that belonged to the worker, and it was where the salary came from.

Consider how each prior wave actually landed. The calculator removed the arithmetic, not the accountant's judgment. The search engine removed the trip to the library, not the analyst's reading. The spreadsheet removed manual recalculation, not the decision about which numbers mattered. In every case the machine took a mechanical step and handed the thinking back. People learned to trust that pattern: tools speed up the work, and the worker stays in charge of the meaning.

Artificial intelligence breaks the pattern. It does not merely retrieve or calculate; it drafts, reasons, summarizes, argues, codes, and critiques. It produces the kind of output that used to be proof that a human had sat down and thought. For the first time, the machine reaches past the muscle and into the cognition itself. That is why it helps to picture AI not as a tool a person points at a task, but as a colleague a person hands a task to: fast, tireless, widely read, occasionally brilliant, occasionally and confidently wrong, and astonishingly cheap. A colleague is not used the way a hammer is. A colleague changes what the day is for.

The distinction is not academic. A person who treats AI as a faster tool reaches for it to speed up the tasks they already do, and gains a little. A person who treats it as a colleague asks a sharper question: which parts of the work should be handed over entirely, and what does that leave for the human to own? The first question saves an afternoon.

The second one rebuilds a career, and it is the question this book keeps returning to.

Knowledge Was the Moat. Now It Isn't.

For most of the modern era, knowing things was a moat. The expert carried scarce knowledge, the tax code, the codebase, the case law, the market, and others paid for access to it. Knowledge took years to accumulate, which is exactly what made it valuable.

The moat protected whole professions. A tax adviser was worth the fee because the code was vast and few had mastered it. A doctor was trusted partly because medical knowledge sat behind years of training and locked library doors. A consultant sold, in no small part, the fact of having read what the client had not. In each case the scarce thing was the knowledge itself, and the person who held it could charge for the holding.

When the answer to almost any question is one good prompt away, the scarce thing is no longer the knowledge. It is knowing which question to ask, whether the answer that comes back is right, and what to do about it. Knowledge is becoming a commodity; judgment is becoming the product. The professional who built an identity on knowing more than the people nearby is about to find the gap narrowing, and the premium quietly moving somewhere else.

From Effort to Outcome

Work used to be paid, mostly, by effort and time and banked knowledge, by showing up and applying what one knew, hour after hour. The effort was visible, and the effort was the point. A junior who stayed late was investing; a senior who had logged thousands of hours was worth more for having logged them.

When the effortful part becomes cheap, no one wants to pay for effort anymore; they want the outcome. The hours spent are becoming invisible; the result is becoming everything. This is liberating for those who are good at producing results, and unsettling for anyone whose professional identity is built on how hard and how long they work. "I put in the time" is starting to sound less like a virtue and more like an admission.

The shift is uncomfortable because effort has always doubled as proof. A long document looked like work; a dense analysis looked like rigour; a late night looked like commitment. When a machine produces the long document in a minute, the proof dissolves, and the only thing left to value is whether the result was right, useful, and wise. That is a harder thing to demonstrate, and a more honest one, and it rewards a different kind of person than the old system did.

The Turing Trap

There is a specific trap waiting here, and many people walk straight into it. The economist Erik Brynjolfsson calls it the Turing Trap. The Turing test asks whether a machine can imitate a human; the trap is building, or becoming, something whose entire value is imitating what the machine can already do. The instinct under threat is to get faster at the very thing AI now does, to beat it at its own game. That instinct points in exactly the wrong direction.

Anyone who defines their value as doing the thing AI is learning to imitate has stepped directly into its path. The escape is the opposite of imitation: to become the human the machine makes more necessary, the one who frames the question, owns the judgment, and is accountable for the call. The goal is not to be faster than the machine at the machine's work; it is to be valuable at the work the machine makes more important.

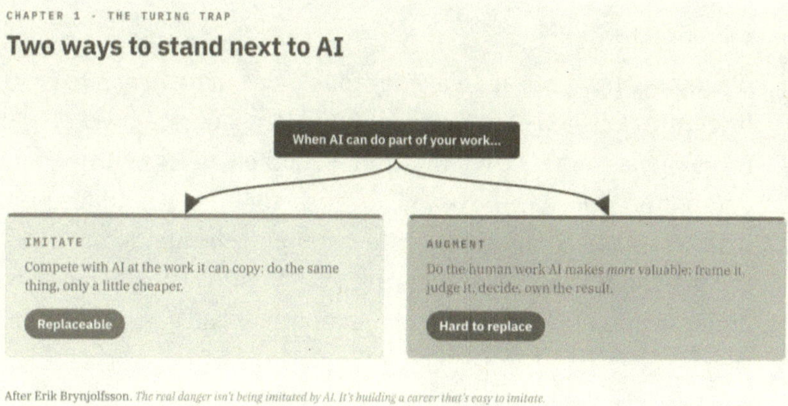

Figure 1.1 *The Turing Trap: imitation makes a person replaceable; augmentation makes them hard to replace.*

There is a hopeful reading of all this, and it is the one worth holding onto. Every task the machine absorbs is a task a person no longer has to spend a working life on. The threat and the opportunity are the same event seen from two sides, and which side a person ends up on is mostly a matter of what they do next. AI is not another icon to add to a toolbar and forget. It behaves less like a tool and more like a new colleague, and a colleague changes the job whether it is welcome or not. The rest of this book is about changing it on purpose, and it begins with an uncomfortable truth: the disruption is not waiting for permission, and it is not impressed by anyone's résumé.

IN PRACTICE

A senior copywriter at an agency took pride in turning a messy brief into polished copy overnight; the long hours were the proof of his worth. When the studio adopted an AI writing tool, a junior produced three usable drafts before lunch, and his first instinct was to compete: to write faster and cleaner, to out-draft the machine. That was the Turing Trap in miniature, exhausting and unwinnable, and it cost him a month of bad sleep before he saw it.

What still required him was the part the tool could not do: deciding which of the three drafts answered the client's unspoken fear, and standing behind that call in the room. The drafting had been the effort he was paid for; the judgment was the outcome they were paying for. He stopped racing the tool and started owning the decision, and the hours he used to spend proving his effort went into the one thing the machine could not supply. Within a quarter he was worth more than before, not less.

IN SHORT

- Past technologies were tools that automated the muscle of knowledge work; AI reaches for the thinking itself.
- Knowing things is no longer the moat: judgment is becoming the product.
- Value is moving from effort to outcome; the hours spent are becoming invisible.
- The Turing Trap: competing with AI at imitation is a losing game; the way out is to become the human it makes more necessary.

ASK YOURSELF

1. What is a person currently paid to know, and how long until a good prompt could surface the same thing?
2. Where does the pay go to effort (hours, busyness), and where to outcomes someone would buy regardless of how long they took?
3. If AI joined the team as a colleague on Monday, which task would go to it first, and what would that free a person to do?
4. Where is someone competing with AI at imitation, and what would moving to the augment side of that line look like?

CHAPTER TWO

Why Smart People Still Get Disrupted

Disruption does not come first for the careless or the junior. It comes first for the capable, and it arrives disguised as a series of perfectly reasonable thoughts. The most skilled person in a room is rarely failing to keep up; that is precisely what makes the exposure so hard to see. Intelligence and credentials rest on a hidden assumption: that the game stays roughly the same. When the game changes, the very things that made a person excellent can become the things that hold them in place. There are four ways it happens.

The comfort trap. When a person is good at something, they stop asking whether it still matters. Competence is comfortable, comfort is quiet, and quiet is exactly where the news that the ground has moved gets missed. The most dangerous sentence in a career is "this is just how it's done." It feels like wisdom and acts like a blindfold, because the more reliably a method has worked, the less anyone in the room thinks to question it.

The experience trap. Experience is compressed pattern recognition, thousands of repetitions teaching a person what works, and it is priceless right up until the pattern changes. Then experience becomes a confident map of a country that no longer exists. The veteran "knows" a task takes three days because it always has; the newcomer who never learned that rule simply asks the model and has a draft by lunch. The veteran's experience is not wrong about the past. It is just no longer a guide to the present.

The certification trap. A credential certifies that, on a particular set of days, a person knew a particular body of knowledge. It is a photograph, not a subscription. Degrees and licenses signal yesterday's competence, and the half-life of competence is shrinking. Some credentials are real gates, and a surgeon should be licensed, but even inside the gate, the work itself is being rewritten, and the letters after a name do nothing to slow that down.

The "too senior" trap. Seniority usually means a person has climbed away from hands-on production into coordination, review, and judgment-by-meeting. Some of that is the durable human work. But a great deal of senior work is coordination overhead, moving information between people, and that is exactly what AI compresses. Being expensive is not the same as being irreplaceable. Sometimes it is the reason a person becomes the line item someone circles.

Why Success Becomes a Liability

Every one of these traps is fed by success. The better the old approach worked, the more a person's income, identity, and reputation are wired into it, and the more it costs to admit it is fading. Sunk cost is not only money; it is self-image. The expert has the most to unlearn and the most reason not to. Disruption skips the beginner and takes the master, because the beginner has nothing to defend.

There is a quiet psychology underneath it. People do not weigh the future neutrally; they protect the story they have told about themselves. A person who has spent fifteen years becoming the best at something does not want a world in which that skill is worth less, so they find reasons to believe it is not happening. The reasons are usually true and beside the point: the machine does make mistakes, it does lack context, it is not as good as the best human. None of that stops the ground from moving. It just makes the moving easier to ignore.

A concrete version of this plays out constantly. A brilliant senior analyst, the one everyone trusts with the quarterly model, has spent a decade becoming fast and precise at building it by hand. A new tool now assembles the same model in minutes. The analyst's instinct, honed by every previous challenge, is to prove they are still faster and more careful, and for a while they are. But the firm does not need the model built more carefully; it needs someone to decide what the model means and what to do about it. The decade of skill was real, and it was aimed at the part that just became cheap. The ones who get caught are almost never the ones who could not do the work. They are the ones who did the wrong work superbly.

The Question That Reveals Exposure

There is a clean way to see whether a role is exposed. Take any task and ask one question: does AI automate it, or augment it? Automation means the task can be done without the person; the person is the cost to be removed. Augmentation means it is done better with the person; the machine amplifies what only they bring.

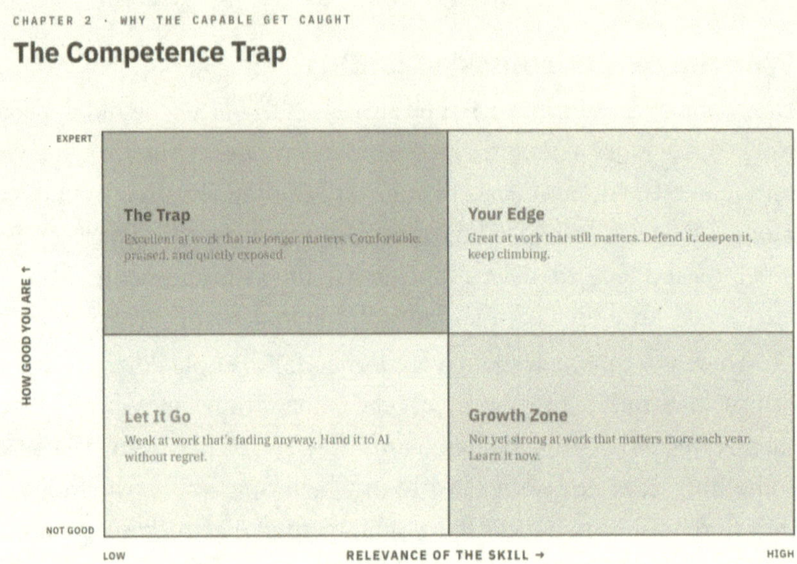

Figure 2.1 *The Competence Trap: how good a person is on the vertical axis, the relevance of the skill on the horizontal.*

The same tool sits on both sides of that line, depending on how it is used and where a person stands. A model that writes the whole report automates the writer who only assembled facts; the same model augments the writer who brings judgment, voice, and a point of view the facts cannot supply. Two people with the same job title can be on opposite sides of the line, and often do not realize it until the org chart makes it plain.

The work, then, is not to avoid AI but to keep relocating, task by task, from the side where it replaces a person to the side where it multiplies them. That is a continuous act, not a one-time decision, because the line itself keeps moving. The competence trap catches the people who plant a flag on the automate side, call the busyness value, and stop checking the map. Smart people are not immune to this. They are more prone to it, because their competence is the very thing that makes the flag feel safe.

Intelligence is not a force field. The disrupted are rarely the people who could not keep up; they are the people who did not believe they had to. The first real skill of escaping disruption is not technical at all: it is the willingness to look hard at one's own competence and ask whether it still points where the value is going. That willingness has a posture and a method, and they are the subject of the next chapter.

IN PRACTICE

A tax accountant with twenty years of practice was the fastest in her firm at preparing returns, a quiet point of pride, and a textbook comfort trap. Her certifications were current and her experience told her exactly how long each return should take, so none of it warned her when the firm's new software began drafting the routine returns automatically. The speed she was proud of was precisely the automatable part, and for three weeks she found reasons the tool did not really threaten her: it missed nuances, it did not know the clients, it was not as careful as she was. All true, and all beside the point.

Only when she listed her week and asked of each task whether AI replaced or amplified her did the picture turn over. The preparation was being automated, while the work she had undervalued, talking an anxious client through a messy year and catching the judgment call no software flags, was the part being amplified. The traps had not made her less skilled. They had simply aimed her skill at the wrong half of the job, and the fix was not to work harder at the fading half but to move her weight to the other one.

IN SHORT

- Disruption often takes the competent first, not the weak: competence hides exposure.
- Four traps catch the capable: comfort, experience, certification, and seniority.
- The better the old approach worked, the harder it is to let go; success becomes a liability.
- One test reveals exposure: does AI automate a task or augment it? The work is to keep moving toward the augment side.

ASK YOURSELF

1. Which of the four traps (comfort, experience, certification, seniority) is most alive in a given career, and what evidence is being waved away?
2. Which prized skill may be certifying yesterday's competence, and what does its current version look like?
3. For the three biggest weekly tasks, is AI more likely to automate each or augment it?
4. Which automatable task gets done because it feels productive, and what could fill the time it would free up?

CHAPTER THREE

Why a Fixed Plan Fails and an Agile Mindset Wins

When people finally accept that AI is coming for part of their work, the instinct is to make a Plan: a serious one, with a syllabus and a credential at the end. It feels responsible. It is also, most of the time, a way to lose.

Why the Plan Feels Safe and Isn't

A plan is a bet on a fixed target. It assumes the ground that is solid today will still be solid in two years, and that a person can walk straight to it. But the target moves faster than any plan can chase. The "safe" skill chosen today may be absorbed into a single AI feature before the course is finished.

Prompt engineering is the cautionary tale. For a brief moment it was the hot, eminently plannable skill: courses, certificates, job titles, the works. Then the models got better at understanding plain language, and much of the craft quietly evaporated, because the thing it optimized for stopped being hard. Anyone who had bet a two-year plan on it was retraining for a role that was disappearing as they trained. A rigid plan in a fast-moving environment is just a detailed map of terrain that will not hold still.

What beats a fixed plan is not the absence of one. It is a posture borrowed from software, called agile: work in short cycles. Try something small, see what happens, adjust, and go again. It replaces prediction with iteration. In a world that cannot be forecast, the person who runs ten small experiments will out-learn the person who spends a year executing one large guess, because the experimenter is collecting evidence about the actual present while the planner is still acting on a guess about the past.

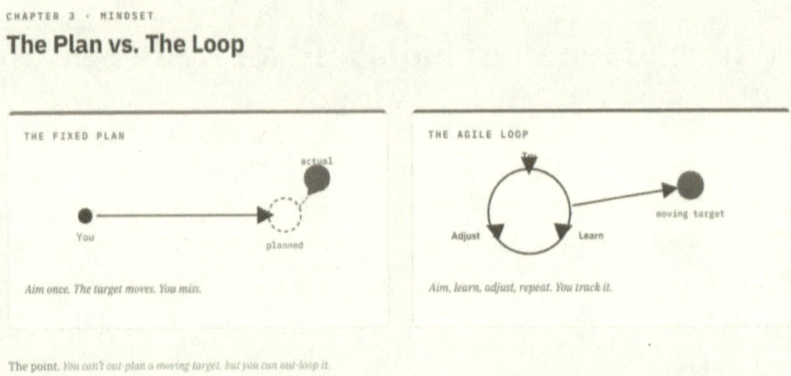

Figure 3.1 *A fixed plan aims once at a moving target; an agile loop tracks it.*

A Capability, Not a Title

There are two ways to hold a career. One is a title: I am a copywriter, an analyst, a database administrator, and a person's worth is the title and the expertise stacked beneath it. The other is a capability: someone who can figure out what is needed and learn it.

The title feels sturdier and is in fact far more fragile, because when the role wobbles, a person's whole sense of who they are wobbles with it. The capability travels; it survives the death of any particular skill because it was never anchored to one. This is the difference the psychologist Carol Dweck drew between a fixed and a growth mindset, and in an age of disruption it stops being a poster on a wall and becomes a survival trait. Skills are temporary now; the ability to acquire them is the only durable asset, so it is the one worth building an identity on.

Make Failure Small

Agile people are not braver than everyone else; they have simply made failure cheap. An experiment that costs an afternoon and teaches something is not a failure; it is a data point bought at a discount. The trick is to shrink the bet until being wrong is affordable, so it can happen often and early.

Trying a new tool on one real task this week, not someday, costs an hour if it fails and buys an edge if it does not, while everyone else is still reading about it. "Fail fast, fail cheap" is not a licence to be careless; it is permission to start before the moment feels ready, which, in a moving environment, is the only moment that ever comes. The people who wait for certainty are choosing to learn last.

Curiosity Outlasts Fear

Fear is a real and rational motivator; the fear of being left behind will get a person off the couch. But fear is poor long-term fuel. It produces anxiety, brittle effort, and a quiet hatred of the very thing a person most needs to befriend, and it burns out long before the change is over.

The ones who stay ahead for years are almost always the ones who got curious, who poke at the new tool because it is genuinely interesting. Curiosity cannot be manufactured on demand, but it can be fed: follow the parts that fascinate, and let curiosity carry the load that fear cannot hold for long. A person who finds the work interesting will out-last a person who only finds it frightening, every time.

None of this requires a personality transplant. Curiosity here is small and practical: a willingness to open the tool and see, to ask what it would do with a real problem, to be a little delighted when it surprises. The people who manage it are not unusually brave or unusually technical. They have simply decided that the change is more interesting than threatening, and that decision, repeated week after week, is most of what separates the people who stay ahead from the people who fall behind while insisting they are too busy to look.

Centaur or Cyborg?

Experimentation answers a question that cannot be reasoned out from an armchair: how to work alongside AI. Ethan Mollick describes two modes. The centaur divides the labor cleanly: a person sets the strategy, the model drafts; the person decides, it generates. The cyborg blends: person and model trade the work back and forth, line by line, until the seam disappears.

Neither is right in the abstract. Some tasks reward a centaur's clean handoff; others reward a cyborg's blur. A long report might want the centaur, with the human owning the structure and the model filling the sections; a tricky paragraph might want the cyborg, with the two trading sentences until it lands. The only way to find out is to try both on real work, which is exactly what an agile, experimental posture makes easy and a fixed plan never will.

In practice the loop is mundane, which is its strength. A person picks one real task each week, tries it with a model in both modes, keeps what worked, and notes in a line or two what they learned. Over a year that is fifty small experiments and fifty notes, an evidence base about their own work that no course could provide and no plan could anticipate. The compounding is quiet and then sudden: the person who has been looping for a year has not just collected tools, they have rebuilt how they think about their work, while the planner is still partway through the syllabus.

A perfect five-year plan is not the requirement, and could not be written if it were. What is required is a fast, cheap loop and the disposition to keep running it while everyone around is still drafting their plan. That loop is the engine of this book, introduced in full later as the ESCAPE loop. But a loop is only as good as the mind running it, which is why the mind comes first.

IN PRACTICE

A marketing manager, rattled by a product demo, nearly enrolled in a six-month "AI for Marketers" certificate, the responsible-looking plan. On a colleague's nudge he tried something smaller instead: one hour, one real campaign brief, handed to a model to see what came back. The result was mediocre, which was exactly the value, because he now knew where the tool was strong and where it was useless, and he had learned it in an afternoon rather than a semester.

He kept the experiment running every week, each one cheap, each one teaching him a little more about where the line fell. By the time that certificate would have ended, half its syllabus was obsolete, and he had quietly become the person his team came to when they were stuck, not because he had a plan, but because he had a loop. Somewhere around week three he had also started to find the whole thing genuinely interesting, which was what kept the loop running after the initial fear wore off.

IN SHORT

- A fixed plan bets on a fixed target, but the target keeps moving; iteration beats prediction.
- A career held as a capability, someone who can learn what is needed, outlasts one held as a title.
- Small, frequent, cheap experiments out-learn one big bet.
- Curiosity outlasts fear as fuel; trying both centaur and cyborg modes reveals how to work with AI.

ASK YOURSELF

1 Is a professional identity a title ("I am a ____") or a capability ("someone who can learn ____")? What changes when it is rewritten as the second?

2 What is one cheap experiment with an AI tool worth running this week, one that costs an hour and might teach something?

3 Where is the fuel fear, and where curiosity? Which part of this shift is genuinely interesting?

4 On one real task, does a centaur's clean handoff or a cyborg's blend fit better, and why?

CHAPTER FOUR

Why AI Will Not Replace Everyone Equally

"Is AI going to take my job?" sits underneath every conversation about this, usually unspoken. The honest answer is unsatisfying, because it is: it depends which part of the job, and on what the person does next. A job is not one thing that AI takes or leaves. It is a bundle of tasks, and the tasks have very different fates.

The Four Fates of Work

Sorting the work of any job into four piles makes the picture clearer.

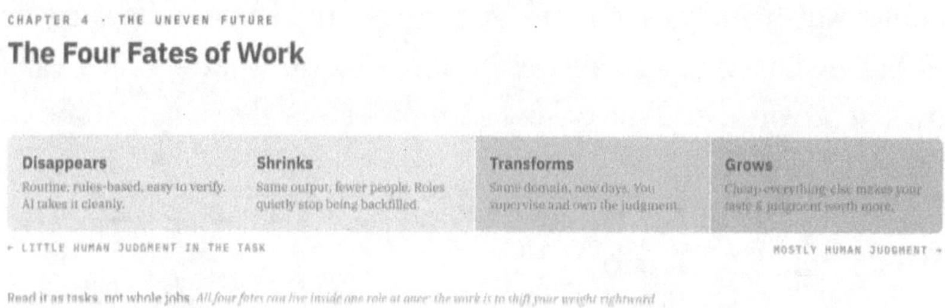

Figure 4.1 *The Four Fates of Work, ordered by how much human judgment the task carries.*

Some work disappears. Tasks that are fully automatable and carry little human premium, routine, rules-based, easy to verify, go first. Basic data entry, simple report generation, the boilerplate sections of every document. When a task is repetitive and the cost of a small error is low, the machine takes it cleanly, and few people miss it once it is gone.

Some work shrinks. Here AI does not remove the human; it means fewer humans produce the same output. A team of eight becomes three; a support floor of fifty handles the same volume with twenty and a model. The work survives; the number of people doing it contracts. This is the quiet fate, the one nobody announces: no dramatic replacement, just a door that stops being opened and a role that stops being backfilled when someone leaves.

Some work transforms. Same domain, different days. The radiologist does not vanish; the job shifts from catching every finding alone to supervising a system that catches them, and owning the hard judgment calls and the conversation with the patient. The developer types less boilerplate and spends more time on architecture and review. The job keeps its name and changes its hours, and the people who thrive are the ones who let it.

And some work grows more valuable. For some work, having AI handle the rest makes the human part worth more, not less. When drafting is cheap, the person with the taste to know which draft is right becomes more valuable. When analysis is instant, the person who knows which analysis matters, and can be trusted with the decision, is in higher demand. AI can raise the ceiling on what a single capable person is worth, and the ceiling rises fastest for the people standing in the right place.

It Is Tasks, Not Jobs

All four fates can live inside one job at the same time: some tasks disappearing while others quietly grow more valuable. That is why "will AI take my job" is the wrong frame. Jobs are bundles; AI unbundles them; the real question is what the bundle looks like after the unbundling, and whether a person has shifted their weight onto the tasks that are rising. No one is a single thing to be kept or cut. Everyone is a portfolio, and portfolios can be rebalanced.

Seen this way, the panic about whole jobs vanishing is mostly a failure of resolution. Almost no job is a single task, and almost no job is all one fate. The useful exercise is not to ask whether a job survives, but to take it apart, name the fate of each piece, and move deliberately toward the pieces that are growing. That exercise is the heart of the practical chapters later in the book.

Take a single familiar role, a marketing coordinator, and run it through the four fates. Formatting the weekly newsletter and pulling the standard analytics: disappearing. The size of the team that pushes out routine posts: shrinking. The work of briefing, reviewing, and directing campaigns: transforming, as more of it becomes directing a model rather than doing the task by hand. And deciding which campaign is worth running at all, reading what the audience actually wants, owning the brand's voice: growing more valuable by the month. One job, four fates at once, and the coordinator's whole future depends on which of the four they spend the next year getting good at.

The Most Reassuring Idea in Economics

People panic at four words: AI is better than me. But "better" in the absolute is not what decides who does the work. Two centuries ago, David Ricardo showed that even when one party is better at everything, both still gain when each concentrates where their relative advantage is greatest. Economists call it comparative advantage, and it is the most reassuring idea in this book.

A simple version makes it concrete. Suppose a senior person is faster than their assistant at both analysis and scheduling. It still does not pay for the senior to do the scheduling, because every hour spent scheduling is an hour stolen from the higher-value analysis. The assistant has a comparative advantage in scheduling even though they are slower at everything, and both come out ahead when the work is split that way.

Now put AI in the role of the faster party. Even in a future where the machine is absolutely better at most things, a person still holds a comparative advantage: the tasks where their relative edge, or simply their relative cost, makes them the right one to do them, and where the machine's effort is better spent elsewhere. The lesson is not "be better than AI at something," which may be impossible. It is: hand AI the work where its advantage is largest, and concentrate where the relative advantage is highest. That is not surrender; it is how the whole economy is about to reorganize, and a person can do it on purpose and early, rather than have it done to them, late.

Why the Timeline Does Not Need Predicting

Nobody knows the speed. Perhaps these shifts land hard within three years; perhaps they grind out over fifteen. Serious people disagree, and the evidence so far is genuinely mixed: real pressure on some roles, little movement yet in the broad employment numbers. Winning that argument is not necessary, which is fortunate, because it cannot be won in advance.

In every version of the timeline, the same people come out ahead: the ones who keep relocating toward work that is rising in value. If disruption is fast, they adapted in time. If it is slow, they spent the extra years compounding an advantage. Adaptability beats prediction, because adaptability pays off in all the futures and prediction pays off in only one. A person who bets everything on a timeline can be right about the year and still be caught; a person who keeps moving is covered no matter when the wave arrives.

So the question was never whether AI replaces a person; it is whether they keep moving to where they are worth more than the machine. That movement can be learned. It has a shape and a method, and the rest of this book is the map. But no one can move toward higher ground without first seeing the terrain, without knowing exactly where the line between human and machine work falls. Drawing that map is where Part Two begins.

IN PRACTICE

A contracts attorney watched all four fates play out across her own desk in a single year. The first-pass review of standard agreements, once billable hours, disappeared into a tool that flagged the risky clauses in seconds, and her team of four associates quietly became two. It would have been easy to read that as the beginning of the end.

But the work did not vanish so much as rearrange. She now spent her time interrogating what the tool flagged, negotiating the terms that mattered, and being the person a client trusted to say "sign this" or "walk away." The model was absolutely better at speed and coverage; she held the comparative advantage in judgment and trust. She stopped competing on the review and concentrated on the call, and stopped asking how many years she had before the change arrived, because it already had, and she was already standing in the part of the job that was growing.

IN SHORT

- "Will AI take my job?" is the wrong question; jobs are bundles of tasks with four fates: disappear, shrink, transform, grow.
- Comparative advantage keeps a person valuable even when AI is absolutely better: hand the machine the weakest tasks, concentrate on the relative edge.
- Predicting the timeline is not necessary: adaptability wins in every version of it.
- The work is to keep shifting weight toward tasks that are rising in value.

ASK YOURSELF

1 Broken into its five to seven main tasks, which fate (disappear, shrink, transform, grow) does each one face?

2 Which "growing" task deserves more time, and what would be dropped to make room?

3 Where is AI absolutely better, yet treated as a threat instead of a handoff, and what should be delegated first?

4 If disruption is slow, what edge could be compounded in the extra years? If it is fast, what will have been worth starting today?

PART TWO

WHAT

What Exactly Is AI Disruption?

Disruption stops being frightening the moment a person can see exactly where the line between human and machine work falls.

CHAPTER FIVE

Mapping the Boundary Between Human and Machine

Part One argued that the disruption is real and falls unevenly. This chapter draws the map: where the line between human and machine actually runs. It matters because most people carry the wrong map in their heads, a neat wall with simple tasks on the machine side and clever tasks safe on the human side. Acting on that map is one of the main ways capable people misjudge their own exposure. The real boundary answers three questions, and three well-known ideas answer them: what shape the line is, why it is shaped that way, and what stays on the human side.

The Shape of the Boundary

Ethan Mollick's image is the place to start: the jagged frontier. AI capability is not a smooth wall but a zig-zagging line. The model drafts a passable contract and then miscounts the words in it; it writes working code and invents a citation that does not exist. Brilliance and uselessness sit side by side.

The figure shows what that means in practice. Tasks above the line are ones AI already handles well; tasks below it still need a human. The surprise is how they sort. Drafting a memo sits above the line, while citing sources reliably sits below it, even though the second feels easier. Because the line zig-zags, intuition about what is hard or easy is a poor guide to what is safe.

The examples multiply once a person starts looking. A model can write a sophisticated marketing email but cannot reliably tell whether the discount it offered is one the company can afford. It can summarize a contract but cannot be trusted to notice the single missing clause that matters most. It can produce ten plausible strategies and has no way to know which one fits this team, this market, this moment. In each pair, the part that looks like the hard, expensive work is the part it does well, and the part that looks like a formality is the part that still needs a human.

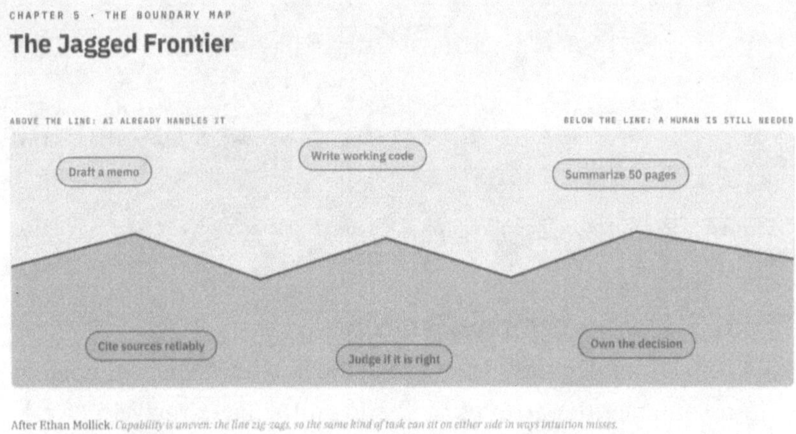

Figure 5.1 *The Jagged Frontier: tasks sort above or below the line in counterintuitive ways.*

Why the Boundary Is Shaped That Way

Moravec's Paradox explains the jaggedness. What is hard for humans is often easy for AI, and what is effortless for humans is often hardest to automate. A computer mastered chess decades before a robot could fold laundry, because chess is formal and laundry is full of physical common sense.

The same inversion runs through knowledge work. The formal, hard-won skills a person is proudest of, like drafting a competent memo, are often the most automatable. The everyday judgment they never think about, like sensing whether the memo's recommendation is wise, is the part that holds.

The practical lesson is to be suspicious of pride. The tasks a person trained longest for, and is most complimented on, are exactly the ones to examine first, because difficulty for a human and difficulty for a machine are not the same thing and often run opposite. The skill that took ten years to master may be the one a model learned overnight, while the thing done without thinking, the judgment call made in a corridor, may be the one no model can touch.

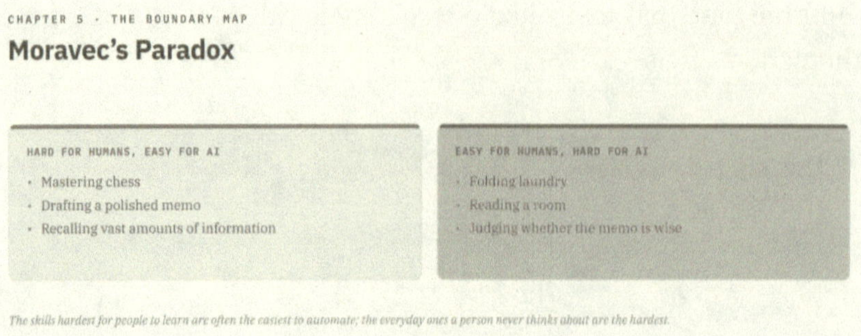

Figure 5.2 *Moravec's Paradox: the skills hardest to learn are often the easiest to automate.*

What Stays on the Human Side

Polanyi's Paradox names what sits below the line. Michael Polanyi put it in a sentence the economist David Autor later revived: "we know more than we can tell." Much human expertise is tacit. A seasoned nurse senses that a patient is about to deteriorate; a negotiator feels the room turn. Neither can fully write down the rule, because there is no tidy rule.

A machine learns from what can be written down, so tacit knowledge resists automation. This is why work that looks unglamorous on paper can sit firmly on the human side of the frontier, and why the largest, most valuable part of expertise is often the part no one can quite explain.

It also explains a common and painful surprise. People often find that the part of a job they assumed was most replaceable, the messy human contact, the judgment calls, the reading of a situation, is the part that holds, while the polished, expert-looking output they were proudest of is the part that moves. The map does not flatter anyone, and that is its value: it shows the ground as it is, not as a résumé would like it to be.

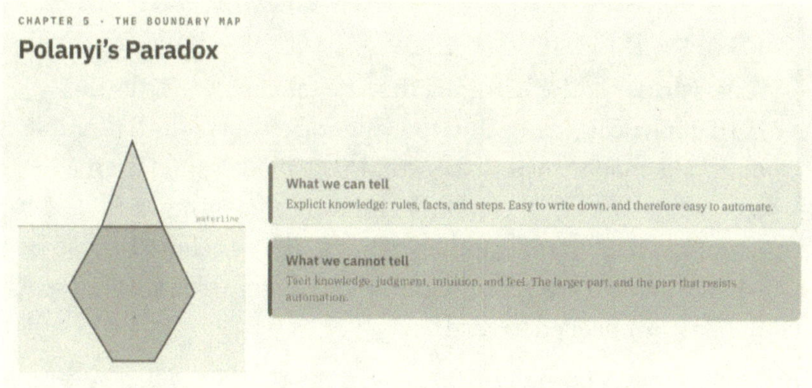

Figure 5.3 *Polanyi's Paradox: most expertise is tacit, and a machine can only learn what can be told.*

Drawing the Map

Put together, the three lenses become a quick test for locating any task. First, which side of the jagged line does it fall on, judged by what AI can actually do rather than by how hard it feels? Second, is it a formal, learnable skill, which tends to automate, or everyday judgment, which tends to hold? Third, does it run on explicit steps that can be written down, or on tacit knowledge that cannot? Run a real job through those three questions and the map stops being abstract. It shows, task by task, where a person is exposed and where they are not, which is exactly what the next chapters build on: what AI can already do, what is fading, and what is rising.

IN PRACTICE

A newspaper editor assumed the safe, human work was the hard analytical writing and the vulnerable work was the simple stuff. The map turned that around. The model could draft a competent analytical column in minutes, the formal and learnable skill, but it could not work a nervous source, sense when a quote felt off, or decide which of three true stories the public most needed to read.

Those were the tacit, effortless-seeming things she had never thought to call skills, and they sat squarely below the frontier. She stopped guarding the long-form drafting, where the line had already moved past her, and put her energy into sourcing and news judgment, where it had not. The byline still carried her name, but the work behind it had relocated to the part of the job a machine could not reach, and her value rose as the drafting got cheaper.

IN SHORT

- The chapter draws a map of where the human and machine boundary falls; the everyday mental map, a neat wall, is wrong.
- Jagged Frontier (the shape): the boundary zig-zags, so intuition about what is hard or easy misleads.
- Moravec's Paradox (the why): formal, hard-won skills automate easily, while everyday judgment resists.
- Polanyi's Paradox (what stays human): tacit knowledge, what we know but cannot tell, cannot be automated.
- Locate any task with three questions: which side of the line, formal or judgment, explicit or tacit.

ASK YOURSELF

1 Taking one real task, does it sit above the frontier (formal, rule-like) or below it (tacit, judgment-laden)?

2 Which prized skill feels hard but is really pattern-matching, and which overlooked one rests on common sense?

3 Where has the frontier already moved past a task that is still being defended?

4 What tacit knowledge does a person hold that they have never thought to call a skill?

CHAPTER SIX

What AI Can Already Do Better, Faster, or Cheaper

It is worth taking an honest inventory of the present, not the hype. Across writing, research, coding, analysis, design, and operations, AI can already produce a competent first pass faster and cheaper than a person. It is not perfect, and that is not the point. The point is that "competent first pass, instantly, at almost no cost" changes the economics of any task built on first passes, which is most knowledge work.

A quick tour makes the point. In writing, AI produces serviceable drafts, summaries, and translations. In research, it gathers and synthesizes faster than any person can read. In coding, it writes functioning code from a description and explains code it did not write. In analysis, it surfaces patterns and drafts the commentary that goes with them. In design and operations, it generates options and handles routine exceptions. None of it is flawless, and all of it is improving, but the floor is already high enough to change what a competent first pass is worth, which is almost nothing.

AI as a Junior Colleague

The most useful way to hold this is to picture AI as a tireless junior colleague: an assistant, a research aide, a coach, a co-worker. It drafts, gathers, summarizes, generates options, and explains things patiently. Like a bright junior, it is fast and broad but needs direction and checking, and it does not know what matters or when it is wrong.

That reframes the value of a senior person. It is no longer in doing the junior work, which the machine now does in seconds, but in directing it and verifying it: setting the right task, spotting the confident error, and standing behind the result. The work moves up a level rather than disappearing.

This is why the people who get the most from AI are often not the most technical, but the best at delegating. Anyone who has managed a capable junior already knows the move: give a clear brief, expect a strong but imperfect first attempt, and apply judgment to what comes back. The manager who rewrites every line gets little leverage; the one who briefs well and reviews sharply multiplies their output. The instincts that make a good manager of people now make a good user of machines.

It is worth being precise about the limits, too, because the analogy can flatter the machine. A junior human learns from being corrected and stops repeating a mistake; today's models will often make the same confident error again tomorrow. A junior knows what they do not know; the model does not, and answers just as fluently when it is wrong as when it is right. The directing and verifying are not optional polish. They are the part that keeps the whole arrangement from quietly going wrong.

Prediction vs. Judgment

The clearest lens on all of this comes from the economists Ajay Agrawal, Joshua Gans, and Avi Goldfarb. Strip AI down and it is a prediction machine. It makes prediction, the next word, the likely answer, the probable outcome, abundant and cheap. What it does not supply is judgment: deciding what matters, what to optimize for, and what to do when the stakes are high or the prediction is uncertain.

The split is easy to miss because the two are bundled together in how people talk about decisions. A doctor "diagnoses," a manager "decides," an analyst "calls it," and each word hides a prediction step and a judgment step inside it. AI is pulling the two apart. It can increasingly supply the prediction, the likely diagnosis, the probable outcome, the forecasted number, while the judgment, what to weigh, what risk to accept, what to actually do, stays with the person who is accountable for being wrong.

This is also why the slogan "AI will replace experts" has the dynamic backwards. The expert's prediction is the part being automated, while the expert's judgment, earned over years and answerable to real consequences, is the part being made more valuable. The future expert does less predicting and more deciding, spending less time producing the answer and more time being the person who can be trusted with it.

That shift sounds like a demotion and is closer to a promotion. Producing the answer was always the laborious part; deciding what the answer means and what to do about it was always the valuable part. AI is taking the labor and leaving the value, which is a strange kind of gift, uncomfortable mainly for anyone who had come to define themselves by the labor.

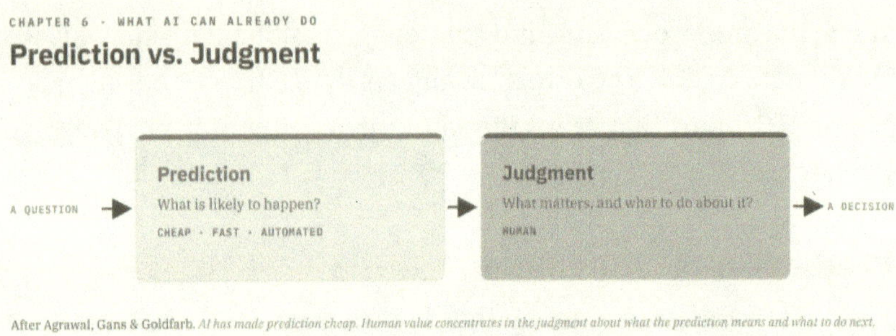

Figure 6.1 *Prediction vs. Judgment: AI makes prediction cheap; humans supply the judgment about what to do.*

When prediction becomes cheap, judgment becomes more valuable, the way cheap coffee makes a good barista's taste matter more, not less. Every task can be split into a prediction part, which can be handed to the machine, and a judgment part, which a person still owns. Learning to see that split inside one's own work is the central skill of this part of the book, and knowing what AI can do is only half the map. The other half is which skills it makes less valuable, and which more.

IN PRACTICE

A developer who had quietly measured her worth in lines of code watched the model write boilerplate faster than she could type. Treated as a junior colleague, it was extraordinary: it scaffolded modules, wrote tests, and explained unfamiliar libraries on demand.

What it could not do was decide which feature was worth building, judge whether the design would survive contact with real users, or own the outage at two in the morning. The prediction had become cheap; the judgment about what to build, and the accountability when it broke, were still hers. She learned to brief the model like a manager rather than race it like a rival, and her job did not shrink so much as move up a layer, from writing the code to deciding what the code should be.

IN SHORT

- AI can already produce a competent first pass faster and cheaper than a person across most knowledge work.
- It behaves like a tireless junior colleague: fast and broad, but needing direction and verification.
- Prediction vs. Judgment: AI makes prediction cheap, so human judgment about what to do becomes more valuable.
- Every task splits into a prediction part to delegate and a judgment part to keep.

ASK YOURSELF

1 For a core task, what is the prediction part (delegable) and what is the judgment part (kept)?

2 Where would treating AI as a junior colleague, directed and verified, change how a week is spent?

3 What confident errors would a person need to catch for the machine's output to be trusted?

4 If prediction is now cheap, where does a person's judgment become the scarce, valuable thing?

CHAPTER SEVEN

What Skills Are Becoming Less Valuable

Naming the fading work plainly is not meant to frighten, but to redirect. The skills losing value share a clear signature: they are repeatable, low in judgment, and easy to verify. That is precisely the profile of work a cheap, instant prediction machine does well.

Before the list, a word on why this is worth facing at all. It is tempting to skip the chapter on fading skills, the way one skips bad news, and get to the encouraging part. But a person cannot move toward rising work without first being honest about which current strengths are quietly losing value. The list that follows is not a verdict on anyone. It is a mirror, and mirrors are most useful precisely when a person would rather not look.

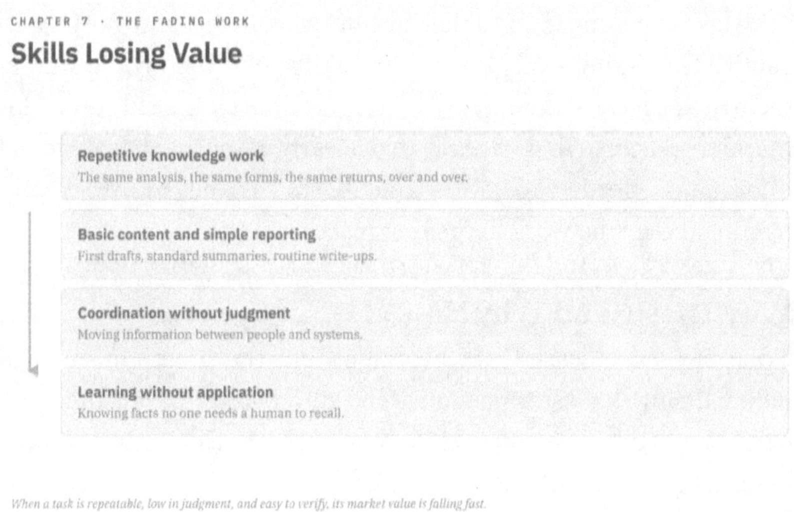

Figure 7.1 *The fading work: skills that are repeatable, low in judgment, and easy to verify.*

Repetitive knowledge work. The same analysis, the same forms, the same returns, produced over and over. The repetition that once justified a salary is now the part most easily handed off.

Basic content and simple reporting. First drafts, standard summaries, routine write-ups: the commodity layer of writing, where competent and instant is now the baseline rather than an achievement.

Coordination without judgment. Moving information between people and systems, the human-router role. When the routing carries no real decision, it is among the first things software absorbs.

Learning without application. Knowing facts that no one needs a human to recall. Memorized expertise, detached from the judgment to apply it, loses its scarcity the moment the facts are a prompt away.

What unites the four is not difficulty but verifiability. A task that can be checked against a clear right answer is a task a machine can be trained to do and trusted to repeat. That is why brilliance is no protection here: a superb version of an easily verified task is still an easily verified task. The work that holds its value tends to be the work where "right" is contested, where the answer depends on context and judgment, and where being accountable for the call is itself the job.

This is the uncomfortable heart of the chapter, and worth stating gently. The fading skills are not bad skills, and the people who hold them are not lesser. They simply bet their time on the side of the line a machine reached first. Seeing that clearly is not a defeat; it is the information needed to move, and moving is the entire reason for naming the fading work in the first place.

Why These, and Why Now

None of these goes to zero overnight, but the premium on each is falling. Being the fastest person at the automatable part is the comfort trap from Part One, now made concrete: a real, valued skill that happens to point at the wrong half of the job.

The natural response to seeing a skill fade is to defend it harder, to become the very best at the thing that is becoming cheap. It rarely works, because no one pays a premium for the best human version of something a machine does adequately at a thousandth of the cost. The more useful response is to ask what the fading task was ever in service of. The researcher was not paid to tabulate, but to inform a decision;

the writer was not paid to produce words, but to change a reader's mind. The fading work was always a means, and the end it served is usually still valuable, often more so.

The mirror of the fading work is the rising work, which is a far better place to stand, and the subject of the next chapter.

IN PRACTICE

A market researcher had built a career on producing clean survey reports: gather, tabulate, summarize, format. For years that was valuable precisely because it was tedious and slow, and he was reliably good at it.

The model now did the tabulating and the first summary in minutes, and his clients noticed. The skills he had honed, the careful assembling and the standard write-up, were exactly the repeatable, verifiable ones losing their premium. What clients still paid for was the part he had treated as an afterthought: telling them which finding should change their decision. The fading work had been his whole identity, and it had become the cheap part of the job, while the afterthought turned out to be the product.

IN SHORT

- Skills losing value share a signature: repeatable, low in judgment, and easy to verify.
- The fading work includes repetitive knowledge work, basic content, coordination without judgment, and learning without application.
- None goes to zero overnight, but the premium on each is falling.
- Being fastest at the automatable part is the comfort trap made concrete.

ASK YOURSELF

1. How much of a typical week is repeatable, low in judgment, and easy to verify?
2. Which valued skill is really speed at the automatable part?
3. Where is coordination being done that carries no real decision?
4. What knowledge is being held that no one any longer needs a human to recall?

CHAPTER EIGHT
What Skills Are Becoming More Valuable

As the automatable layer turns into a commodity, a different set of skills rises in its place: problem framing, judgment, creativity, decision-making, systems thinking, human connection, and the new craft of designing AI workflows. They share a property that the fading skills lack: a machine cannot own them.

The Judgment Gap

One idea ties the rising skills together. AI does the first 80% of a task, the draft, the analysis, the options, and the value concentrates in the last mile it cannot own: which option, whether it is right, what to do about it, and who is accountable for the call.

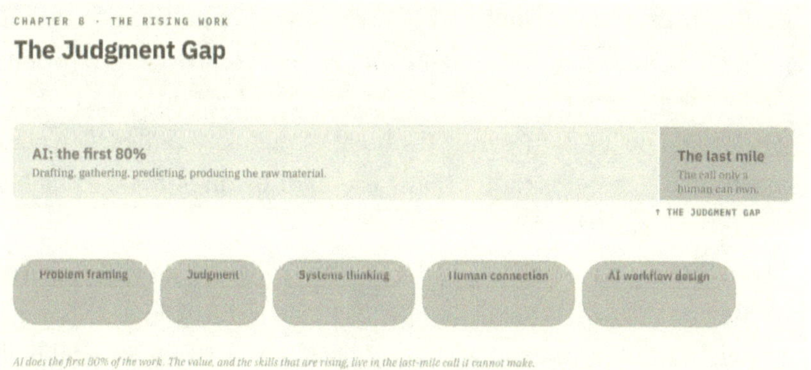

Figure 8.1 *The Judgment Gap: AI does the first 80%; human value is the last-mile call.*

The gap is where the rising skills live. Problem framing decides which 80% gets produced in the first place. Judgment evaluates the output. Decision-making closes it. Human connection carries it to the people who must act. And AI workflow design, the genuinely new skill, orchestrates the tools so the first 80% is reliable enough to build on.

A worked example shows the gap in motion. A model can analyze a customer dataset and produce twelve charts in seconds, which is the first 80%. The last mile is everything that makes it matter: deciding which two charts answer the question the business actually has, noticing the one result that contradicts the strategy and being willing to say so, and recommending an action someone will be accountable for. The charts are abundant and nearly free. The judgment about which chart should change a decision is scarce and highly paid, and the gap between the two is widening.

The size of the gap varies by task, and learning to feel its width is itself a skill. For a routine email the gap is small, and the model's draft is almost the whole job. For a strategic decision under uncertainty the gap is enormous, the analysis is the easy tenth, and the judgment is everything. A person who can sense, task by task, how much of the value lives in the last mile is a person who knows where to spend their scarce attention.

Systems Thinking and Seeing the Whole

As AI absorbs individual tasks, the scarce human ability becomes seeing how tasks connect into outcomes. Almost anyone can prompt a model for a single piece; few can design the whole flow, find where it breaks, and tie it to something the business actually values. The person who thinks in systems rather than tasks ends up directing the machines instead of competing with them.

Designing the workflow is the genuinely new craft, and it is worth naming on its own. It means knowing which parts of a job to hand to a model, in what order, and with what checks, so that an unreliable first 80% becomes a dependable output. It is part editing, part systems design, part quality control, and almost no one was trained for it, which is exactly why it is becoming valuable. The person who can build a reliable pipeline out of an unreliable tool is worth far more than the person who can only prompt it once and hope.

Put the rising skills together and a pattern appears. Every one of them is about steering rather than producing: choosing the problem, judging the output, connecting it to people, and building the system that makes it reliable. The machine produces; the valuable human steers. A career that moves from producing toward steering is a career moving up the judgment gap, toward the part of the work that grows more valuable as the machine gets better.

Human Connection

Trust, persuasion, care, and reading a room are the tacit, relational skills from the human side of the frontier, and they rise for two reasons. They cannot be automated, and in a world flooded with cheap content, a trusted human becomes scarcer and therefore more valuable.

There is a paradox worth sitting with here. The more capable the machines become, the more the distinctly human things appreciate. When anyone can generate a competent document, the scarce and valuable acts are the ones a document cannot perform: earning trust, having a hard conversation, taking responsibility, caring visibly about the outcome. The technical frontier and the human premium move in opposite directions, which is why the rising skills are so often the ones that have nothing to do with the technology at all.

These skills are learnable, and Part Six turns them into a method. But before the method comes a profile: what a resilient person actually looks like.

IN PRACTICE

A consultant noticed that her juniors could now generate in an afternoon the analysis decks that once took a team a week. The decks were no longer the value, and pretending otherwise would have fooled no one for long.

What the client paid her for sat squarely in the judgment gap: framing the real question behind the brief, knowing which of the model's twelve charts actually mattered, and sitting across the table to make a recommendation she would stake her name on. She spent less time reviewing slides and more on framing, on the final call, and on designing the workflow that let the juniors and the model produce a reliable first 80%. Her rate went up, not down, because she had moved to the part of the work the speed of the machine made scarcer.

IN SHORT

- As automatable work commoditizes, framing, judgment, decision-making, systems thinking, connection, and AI workflow design rise.
- The Judgment Gap: AI does the first 80%; the value is the last-mile call it cannot own.
- Systems thinking, seeing how tasks connect into outcomes, turns a person into the one directing the machines.
- Human connection rises because it cannot be automated and trusted humans grow scarcer.

ASK YOURSELF

1. On a recent piece of work, where exactly was the last-mile call that AI could not own?
2. Which rising skill (framing, judgment, systems thinking, connection, workflow design) is the weakest, and worth building?
3. Where could a person design the whole workflow rather than just prompt for a piece?
4. Which relationships and sources of trust would be worth investing in now?

CHAPTER NINE

What Makes a Person AI-Resilient

There is no single safe skill to acquire and bank. Resilience in the face of AI is a profile: a set of dispositions that let a person keep moving as the frontier shifts. Six of them do most of the work.

It is worth pausing on why the answer is a profile and not a list of safe jobs. People want a name: tell me the role that is future-proof. But there is no future-proof role, only future-proof dispositions, because every role is a moving bundle of tasks. What protects a person is not the chair they sit in but the way they meet change, and that way can be described, practiced, and strengthened. The six traits below are that description.

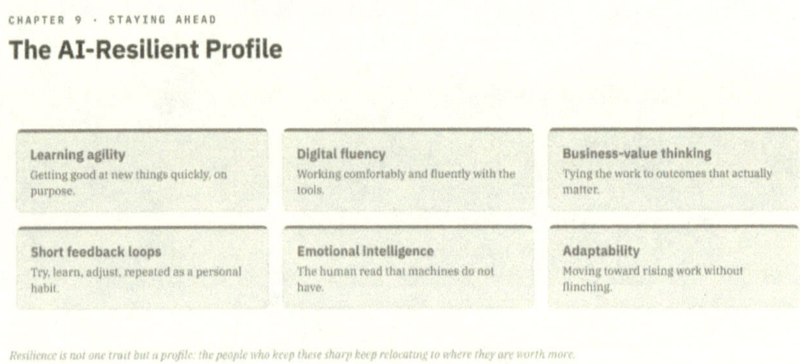

Figure 9.1 *The AI-resilient profile: six habits that let a person keep relocating.*

Learning agility. Getting good at new things quickly, on purpose. It is the meta-skill, because in a world where any specific skill is temporary, the ability to acquire the next one is the durable asset.

Digital fluency. Working comfortably with the tools, neither fearing them nor fetishizing them. Fluency is not about coding; it is about knowing what the tools can do and reaching for them by instinct.

Business-value thinking. Tying the work to outcomes that matter, so effort lands where it actually pays. The person who can connect a task to value is hard to automate and harder to replace.

Short feedback loops. The personal habit of try, learn, adjust, run again. It is the same loop from Part One, now a way of life rather than a one-time response, and it is the engine that keeps the other traits current.

Emotional intelligence. The human read that machines do not have: empathy, trust, the sense of what is really going on between people. As content gets cheap, this gets dear.

Adaptability. Moving toward rising work without flinching when the old work fades. It is less a skill than a willingness, and it is what turns the other five into action.

A Profile, Not a Single Skill

None of these is exotic, and no one of them is enough alone. Resilience is the set kept sharp together, because it is the combination that lets a person relocate again and again as the ground moves.

The traits are worth keeping together because they reinforce one another. Learning agility is faster when feedback loops are short, because each loop is a lesson. Digital fluency makes the experiments cheaper to run. Business-value thinking points the agility at things that matter rather than novelty for its own sake. Emotional intelligence makes the whole thing land with other people, and adaptability is the willingness that turns all of it into movement. Strengthen one and the others get easier; neglect one and it drags on the rest.

Building the profile is less daunting than it sounds, because these are habits more than talents. Short feedback loops are a calendar choice: one small experiment a week. Digital fluency grows from use, not study. Business-value thinking is a single question asked often enough that it becomes automatic: what is this actually for? None of it requires a sabbatical or a degree. It requires the willingness to keep doing small things, on purpose, while the ground keeps moving, which is the whole disposition this book is trying to build.

It helps to remember why a profile beats a single skill. One safe skill is a bet that a particular task stays valuable, and that bet keeps losing as the frontier moves. A profile is a bet on the ability to keep finding the next valuable thing, which is the one bet that pays off no matter how the frontier moves. The resilient person is not the one who guessed right about which skill to learn. It is the one who never stopped being able to learn the next one.

There is one more thing the profile makes possible, and it is the quiet point of the whole book. A person who holds these six habits stops meeting each new tool as a threat to be survived and starts meeting it as terrain to be explored. Much of the fear around AI comes from feeling stuck in place while the ground moves. The cure is not a guarantee that any particular skill is safe, because none is. The cure is the earned confidence that whatever the ground does next, a person can move with it, a confidence that is not bravado but the quiet by-product of having relocated successfully once or twice and then trusting oneself to do it again.

Part Two has now drawn the map: where the boundary falls, what AI can already do, which skills are fading, which are rising, and who tends to stay ahead. The next question is when. How fast does this land, and how can a person read the early signals in their own career? That is Part Three.

IN PRACTICE

A small-business owner with no technical background turned out to be more AI-resilient than the specialists who worked for her. She was not fluent with the tools at first, but she learned fast, ran cheap experiments most weeks, and judged everything by whether it helped a customer or the bottom line.

When a new tool appeared, she did not ask whether it threatened her; she asked what it could do for the business and tried it that week. The specialists knew more, and several of them spent their energy explaining why the tools were not ready. She adapted faster, and in a landscape that keeps shifting, the second thing mattered more than the first. Her profile, not any single skill, was what kept her ahead.

IN SHORT

- Resilience is a profile, not a single safe skill.
- Its six habits: learning agility, digital fluency, business-value thinking, short feedback loops, emotional intelligence, adaptability.
- Short feedback loops keep the other traits current; adaptability turns them into action.
- The combination, kept sharp, is what lets a person relocate again and again.

ASK YOURSELF

1. Across the six traits, which two are strongest, and which two are the gap?
2. What would a standing habit of short feedback loops look like in an ordinary week?
3. When a new tool appears, is the first question "does this threaten me" or "what can it do for the work"?
4. Where is knowing more being mistaken for adapting faster?

PART THREE

WHEN

When Will AI Disruption Hit You?

The date AI reaches a particular job is unknowable; the direction it is travelling is not, and that is enough to act on.

CHAPTER TEN

The Honest Timeline of Disruption

The question underneath every conversation about AI is a question about time. When does it reach my job? People want a date, and the people who sell certainty are happy to supply one. The honest answer separates two things that usually get tangled together: the direction of the change, which is fairly clear, and the speed of it, which nobody knows. Most predictions fail because they bet everything on the speed. This chapter offers a timeline that is honest about both.

It is worth being precise about what the question even means. "When will AI hit my job" sounds like a request for the date of a single event, a door closing. But disruption almost never arrives as one event. It arrives as a gradual reweighting of a role, task by task, until the job a person does in three years is meaningfully different from the one they do today, often without a single dramatic moment. The honest question is not when the job ends but when it changes, and by how much, and that change is usually already underway by the time anyone thinks to ask.

Two Lies About Timing

Two stories compete for attention, and both are wrong. The first is the hype: everything changes next year, every job gone by Tuesday, the future arriving all at once. It sells newsletters and conference tickets, and it produces panic, which is a poor state for making good decisions. The second is the comfort: nothing will really change, not in any working life that matters, the tools are toys, the fuss will pass. It sells reassurance, and it produces complacency, which is worse.

The truth sits in an uncomfortable middle that neither story finds appealing. Large change is coming, the direction is not really in doubt, and the timing is genuinely uncertain and uneven. A person who believes the hype burns out bracing for a flood that comes slower than promised. A person who believes the comfort is the one standing in the water when it finally rises. The useful stance refuses both lies and holds the discomfort of not knowing the date.

It helps to notice who tells each lie and why. The hype tends to come from those selling the future: vendors, pundits, and anyone whose audience grows with alarm. The comfort tends to come from those invested in the present: incumbents and institutions whose standing rests on the old arrangement continuing. Neither is lying on purpose; each is reporting the world as it would prefer it to be. A person planning a career has no such luxury, and has to look past both interested parties to the unglamorous middle.

The Direction Is Clearer Than the Speed

What is clear deserves to be stated plainly. The capability already exists and keeps improving. The economics strongly favour adoption, because the tools are cheap and the savings are large. And the tasks most exposed are knowable, because the map from Part Two shows where the human and machine boundary falls. The direction of travel, toward more capable tools absorbing more of the routine cognitive work, is about as settled as these things get.

The economics are the engine of that certainty. A tool that does a competent first pass for a fraction of a cent will be adopted, because the pressure to cut cost and move faster is relentless and nearly universal. A single firm that resists can be undercut by a competitor that does not. This is why the direction is so much clearer than the speed: the incentive to adopt is overwhelming and constant, while the friction that slows adoption, habit, regulation, trust, and integration, varies enormously from one place to the next.

What is unclear is everything about the pace. How fast will organizations actually adopt and redesign their work? How will regulation, liability, and professional norms respond? Will capability keep compounding or level off? How quickly can labour markets absorb the shift? None of these has a confident answer, and anyone who offers one is guessing. So the right posture is asymmetric: hold the direction with confidence and hold the timeline with humility.

The discomfort of this asymmetry explains a good deal of bad planning. People crave a date, because a date lets them schedule a response, file it under later, and stop worrying. A clear direction with no date offers no such relief: it asks for a change in behaviour now, with no deadline to procrastinate against and no certainty to justify the effort. So people quietly convert the honest "clear direction, unknown speed" into the dishonest "not proven yet," and use the missing date as permission to do nothing. The missing date is not permission. It is the reason to start, because the one thing worse than preparing a little too early is being surprised far too late.

What Is Already True

The present is real but uneven, and worth describing without exaggeration in either direction. Pilots and tools are everywhere, and there is genuine pressure on specific kinds of work: first-pass content, basic coding, routine analysis, simple support, the more template-driven corners of many roles. Some early-career work, the kind that used to be where juniors learned, is feeling it first.

At the same time, the broad employment numbers have barely moved, and most jobs still look much as they did. The disruption so far is mostly happening at the level of tasks inside jobs, not the wholesale replacement of jobs. Anyone claiming mass displacement has already arrived is overstating the case; anyone claiming nothing has changed is not looking closely. Both the pressure and its limits are real, and an honest read holds them together.

There is a quieter present-tense reality worth naming, too. Even where no job has been lost, the nature of the work is already shifting. People are spending more of the day editing what a machine drafted, checking what it produced, and deciding what to do with it. The title is unchanged and the daily experience is not, and that subtle migration, from producing toward directing and judging, is the leading edge of the disruption, arriving long before any headline does.

The Near and Far Horizons

On the near horizon, the next one to three years, the technology mostly already exists. What changes is not invention but diffusion: tools integrated into workflows, trust slowly built, processes redesigned, people retrained. The bottleneck is organizational, not technical, which is why the visible effects often lag the underlying capability. History rhymes here, because electricity and the personal computer both took years to show up in how work was actually done. Expect task-level disruption to keep spreading, and more roles to be quietly reshaped or thinned.

The lag is not a flaw in the technology; it is how general-purpose technologies always arrive. Factories ran on steam-era layouts for decades after electric motors were available, because capturing the gain meant redesigning the work, not just swapping the power source. Personal computers sat on desks for years before they showed up in the productivity figures, for the same reason. AI is following the pattern: the capability lands first, and the slow reorganization of work around it follows, which is exactly why the present can look calm while the ground has already begun to move.

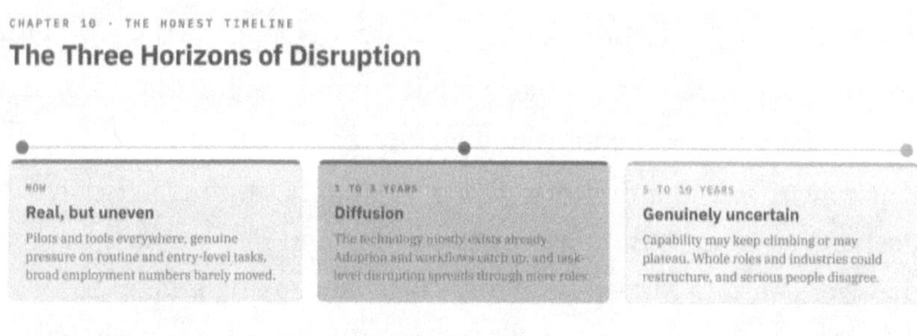

Figure 10.1 *The Three Horizons of Disruption: the direction is clear, the speed is not.*

On the far horizon, five to ten years out, the honest word is uncertain. One plausible future has capability continuing to compound, with whole roles and industries restructured. Another has it reaching a plateau, with changes that are significant but bounded. Serious, informed people genuinely disagree about which is more likely. The wise response to a real fork like this is not to pick a branch and bet the career on it, but to prepare for the range so that either branch can be met.

Disruption Arrives Unevenly

One more honesty is owed about the timeline: it is not a single wave that reaches everywhere at once. It is thousands of smaller waves striking different roles, firms, and regions at different times. A content team may feel it this year while a field-service role feels nothing for a decade. Two people with the same job title at different companies can be on entirely different schedules, depending on each employer's appetite for adoption. This unevenness is why averages mislead. The broad statistics can stay calm for years while specific roles are already being remade, and a person's own timeline depends far more on their particular task and employer than on any national figure.

This is also why comparing oneself to the field average is a mistake. The average says almost nothing about a person's own exposure, which is set by the specific tasks they do and the specific employer they do them for. Two plain questions cut through the noise far better than any statistic: how much of my particular work is becoming automatable, and how quickly is my particular employer moving to adopt? The answers are local, knowable, and far more useful than any figure reported about the economy as a whole.

It is fair to give the optimist's case its due, because it is partly right. Past waves of automation destroyed jobs and also created new ones that were hard to foresee, and there is no law saying this time is wholly different. New roles will appear, some built directly on these tools. But two cautions matter. The new jobs rarely arrive in the same place, at the same time, or for the same people as the ones that vanish, and the transition is where the pain lives. Long-run optimism is cold comfort to a person caught in the short-run gap, which is precisely why preparing beats waiting even if the optimists are proved right in the end.

The practical upshot of all this uncertainty is oddly freeing. Because the exact timeline cannot be known, there is little point waiting for it, and the energy spent debating dates is better spent preparing for the range. A person who accepts that the speed is unknowable stops asking the unanswerable question and starts asking the useful one: what would leave me ready whether this lands in two years or in ten? That question has answers, and they turn out to be the same answers in almost every scenario, which is the quiet gift hidden inside the uncertainty.

Why Waiting Is the Costliest Strategy

Given all this uncertainty, the natural instinct is to wait for clarity before acting. It feels prudent. It is, in fact, the one strategy that loses in every version of the future. If disruption turns out to be fast, the person who waited is caught flat. If it turns out to be slow, the same person has forfeited years of compounding advantage to everyone who started early.

The arithmetic of it is worth making explicit. Starting early costs a few hours a week and some discomfort, and the downside if the disruption never comes is small: a person has merely learned some useful skills ahead of time. Starting late costs a scramble under pressure, with thinner finances and fewer options, and the downside if the disruption does come is severe. A careful person weighs not just the likely outcome but the cost of being wrong in each direction, and here those costs are wildly lopsided. When being early is cheap and being late is ruinous, the decision makes itself, whatever the date turns out to be.

The asymmetry is the whole argument. Adapting early is cheap and reversible: it can be done from a position of employment, with slack to experiment and fail, while the old work still pays the bills. Adapting late is expensive and forced: it happens after the role has thinned, when the finances are tight and the options are few. The cost of moving early is small and the cost of moving late is large, and that imbalance, not any particular forecast, is what should settle the question. The timeline does not need to be predicted. It needs to be prepared for, starting now, from strength. Knowing roughly when the wave is coming raises the next question: how to tell it is approaching one's own shore. That is the work of the next chapter.

IN PRACTICE

A graphic designer watched image-generation tools cross, in under two years, from a curiosity that produced nonsense to something genuinely useful for real work. Most of her studio treated it first as a toy, then as a threat, and spent a great deal of energy arguing about when, exactly, it would be good enough to matter.

She skipped the argument about timing entirely. The direction was obvious and the date was unknowable, and waiting for the date to resolve only meant learning last. She started using the tools on real client work early, while she still had the slack to experiment and fail, and treated the mediocre early results as tuition. By the time the studio accepted the change was real, she was the one who already knew how to direct the tools rather than fear them, and the colleagues who had waited for certainty received their answer at the same moment as everyone else, which was far too late for it to be an advantage.

IN SHORT

- The direction of AI disruption is fairly clear; the speed is genuinely uncertain. Predictions fail because they bet on speed.
- Two lies mislead: the hype (everything changes next year) and the comfort (nothing really changes). The truth is large change on an unknown timetable.
- Today the disruption is mostly at the task level inside jobs; broad numbers have barely moved, though the pressure is real and uneven.

- The near horizon is about diffusion, adoption catching up to capability; the far horizon is genuinely uncertain.
- Waiting loses in every scenario; adapting early, from a position of strength, wins in all of them.

ASK YOURSELF

1. Which of the two lies is more tempting in a given situation, the hype or the comfort, and what does each one conveniently excuse?
2. Which tasks in a role are already feeling task-level pressure, even while the job as a whole looks unchanged?
3. If disruption arrived in three years, would today's preparation look adequate or late?
4. What is the cheapest first step that could be taken now, while there is still slack to take it?

CHAPTER ELEVEN

Early Warning Signals in Your Career

A person rarely receives a clear announcement that their role is being disrupted. The announcement, when it comes, is the reorganization or the layoff, and by then the options are few and the timing belongs to someone else. The skill this chapter builds is reading the earlier, quieter signals, the ones that appear while there is still room to act on them.

Lagging Signals and Leading Signals

A lagging signal confirms what has already happened. The role eliminated, the team cut, the project handed to a tool: useful for understanding the past, useless for changing it. A leading signal appears earlier, and it is easy to dismiss precisely because nothing has gone wrong yet. The entire game is to learn to read leading signals and act on them while acting is still cheap and voluntary.

Signals in the Work

The clearest signals show up in the daily work, for anyone willing to look honestly at their own week.

The work is becoming template-driven. When more of a role fits a repeatable pattern, a shape a tool could be taught to follow, the role is drifting toward the automatable side of the line. Template-driven work is comfortable and it is exposed, and the comfort is what hides the exposure.

A tool now handles a slice of a core task. The moment a model reliably does even a third of the thing a role is built on, the rest tends to follow, because the gap left for a human keeps narrowing as the tool improves. A partial capability today is a strong signal about a fuller capability soon.

Juniors are matching seniors. When a less experienced person armed with AI produces what used to require deep expertise, the premium on that expertise is already being competed away. The scarcity that justified the senior's value is quietly dissolving, even if the title and the salary have not yet caught up.

A single test ties these together. If a capable outsider, handed the team's tools and a week of training, could do a passable version of a task, that task is sending a signal. The test is uncomfortable precisely because it strips away the years of accumulated context that make a person feel irreplaceable, and asks the narrower question the market actually asks: not how hard was this to learn, but how hard is it to replicate now.

The role is being unbundled. When the pieces of a job start being parcelled out, one slice to a tool, another to a cheaper provider, another folded into someone else's role, the job is being unbundled, and unbundling often precedes elimination. A role that is quietly losing its coherent shape is sending one of the clearest signals there is.

Signals in the Team and the Market

Other signals appear just outside the daily work, in how the team and the market behave. AI usually enters an organization sideways rather than by announcement: a colleague quietly using a tool, a pilot in one department, a new feature folded into software everyone already runs. Around the same time, hiring for the role slows, departures stop being backfilled, and the phrase "we can do this with fewer people" starts to surface, often casually, in rooms where budgets are set.

Wider still, the market leaves tracks. Job postings for the role begin to change their wording, asking for AI fluency or quietly rolling three old roles into one. Competitors ship faster with smaller teams. Rates or salaries for the specific skill soften, or the work drifts toward cheaper providers paired with tools. None of these is proof on its own, but a cluster of them is a pattern, and patterns are what leading signals look like before they become headlines.

A concrete pattern recurs across fields. First a tool appears that handles the easy third of a role, and everyone agrees it is a helpful assistant. Then it improves and the assistant quietly does half, and the team that once needed five people delivers the same work with three. No one is dismissed in a dramatic gesture; the two open roles are simply never refilled, and the postings that do appear ask for one person who can do, with tools, what three used to do by hand. By the time this is obvious it has already happened, which is why the earlier and subtler signals are the ones worth training the eye to catch.

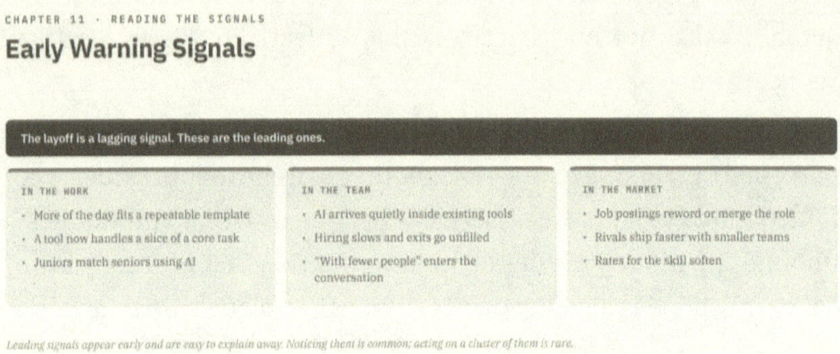

Figure 11.1 *Early Warning Signals: the leading indicators that appear before the layoff.*

Expertise That Is No Longer Scarce, a Role That Is a Workflow

Two deeper signals deserve their own mention, because they cut closer to the bone. The first is the moment a person's hard-won expertise stops being scarce, because a tool now supplies a good-enough version of it on demand. The knowledge is still real, but the market no longer has to pay a premium for access to it, and the basis of that person's value has shifted under their feet even if the paycheck has not yet registered the change.

The second is the moment a role can be described cleanly as a workflow, a sequence of steps that a tool could be slotted into one by one. Roles that reduce neatly to a workflow are on the path to becoming one. Roles that resist the description, because they turn on judgment, relationship, accountability, and the tacit knowledge from Part Two's human side, are far harder to compress, and the difference is worth knowing about one's own work.

Running a Personal Signal Check

Reading signals can be turned into a simple, repeatable habit rather than a vague anxiety. Once a quarter, a person can list the main tasks of their role and mark, honestly, which are becoming more template-driven, which a tool now touches, and which still demand judgment, relationship, or accountability. The same short review can note the quieter context: whether hiring is slowing, whether new tools have appeared in the team, whether the language around the work is changing. Written down, the pattern becomes visible in a way it never is when the signals are felt one at a time and dismissed one at a time. The aim is not to provoke panic but to convert a slow, ambient unease into specific information that can be acted on while there is still time.

Signal or Noise

Not every alarming headline is a signal, and part of the skill is filtering. A flashy demo of a tool doing something impressive once, under ideal conditions, is weak evidence; a tool reliably doing a real slice of actual work, at low cost, is strong evidence. Hype tends to be loud, general, and about the distant future, while a genuine signal tends to be quiet, specific, and about the present. The question to ask of any claim is not whether it is exciting but whether it is already changing how the work in front of a person gets done. The signals that matter are usually the dull ones, visible in the daily grain of a job rather than on a stage.

The Signals Inside

Some of the earliest signals are internal. A creeping boredom as the interesting parts of a job are handed to tools and the residue starts to feel like supervision. A quiet avoidance of the new tools, dressed up as principle. A sense of coasting on reputation rather than being stretched. These feelings are easy to ignore or to moralize, but they are data too, and they often arrive before the external signals do. A person who notices themselves coasting, or flinching from the very tools their field is adopting, has been handed an early and private warning, and what they do with it is theirs alone to decide.

None of these signals, taken alone, is a reason to upend a life. A single soft quarter, a single new tool, a single rewritten posting can mean nothing. The skill lies in the cluster and the trend: several signals pointing the same way over a couple of quarters. One swallow is not a summer, but a sky steadily filling with them is. Reading signals well means neither panicking at the first nor waiting for the undeniable last, but watching the pattern accumulate and acting while the acting is still cheap.

The Trap of Explaining the Signals Away

Every leading signal is easy to rationalize, and the competent are the most gifted rationalizers of all, for the reasons Part One laid out. The tool is not as good as me. The clients still want a human. My situation is genuinely different. Each of these may be perfectly true, and not one of them stops the trend, because the trend does not require the tool to be better than the best human. It only requires it to be good enough, cheap enough, and improving.

And once a real signal is confirmed, the right reaction is motion, not dread. A confirmed signal is good news in one important sense: it has arrived early, while there is still slack, still income, and still time to learn. The person who reads a signal a year before the reorganization is in a far stronger position than the one who learns of the change on the day it lands. Early information is the entire prize, and it is wasted only by those who, having seen the signal, choose to look away.

The discipline, then, is to treat a cluster of signals as information to act on rather than as claims to argue down. Noticing early is worth very little if the noticing is followed immediately by an explanation for why it does not apply. The signals tell a person that the wave is coming. They do not say what to do about it, and the response, whether to upgrade, pivot, or reinvent, depends on reading one's own exposure honestly. That is the subject of the next chapter.

IN PRACTICE

A translator noticed machine translation crossing from laughable to usable for routine documents, while it remained poor at nuance, idiom, and anything high-stakes. The signals were everywhere once she looked: agencies offering lower "post-editing" rates, clients sending machine drafts to "just clean up," and more volume expected for less money.

Many of her peers explained the signals away. The machine could not handle literature, could not catch the cultural subtlety, would never truly replace a human. All true, and all about the wrong tasks. She read the signals instead as a map: the routine, high-volume work was going, and the nuanced, high-trust, high-stakes work was not. She moved her practice toward the second while the first still paid, and kept her income steady while peers who waited watched their rates fall. The signals had been visible to everyone in the field. Acting on them, rather than arguing with them, was the rare part.

IN SHORT

- The layoff is a lagging signal; by then it is too late. The skill is reading leading signals, which appear while there is still room to act.
- Signals in the work: the role becoming template-driven, a tool handling a slice of a core task, juniors matching seniors with AI.
- Signals in the team and market: hiring slowing, "fewer people" talk, more output expected, postings rewording the role.
- Two deeper signals: expertise that is no longer scarce, and a role that can be described as a workflow.
- The competent are the best at explaining signals away; the discipline is to treat a cluster of them as information, not as claims to argue down.

ASK YOURSELF

1. How much of a typical week is becoming template-driven, the kind of pattern a tool could be taught to follow?
2. Where has a tool already started handling a slice of a core task, and what usually happens to the rest?
3. Could the role be described cleanly as a workflow? Which parts resist that description?
4. Which signals are currently being explained away, and what would change if they were treated as information instead?

CHAPTER TWELVE

When to Pivot, Upgrade, or Reinvent

Reading the signals raises the only question that matters: what to do about them. The answer is not a single thing, and it is not, for most people, a dramatic leap. Panic is not a plan, and neither is treating every warning as a reason to start over. There are three responses, scaled to how exposed a role is and how far a person's edge carries, and most of the skill lies in matching the response to the situation.

The Exposure-Advantage Test

A simple test makes the choice clearer. Run the work, not the job title, through two questions. How replaceable is the task, which is its exposure? And how much human edge does it carry, the judgment, trust, relationship, and taste from the human side of the frontier? Two questions produce four responses, and where the bulk of a role lands points to the move.

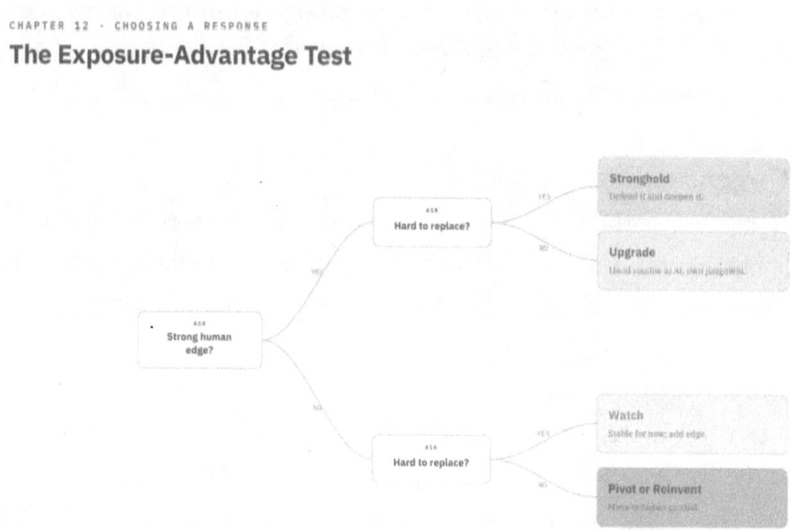

Two questions, four responses. *A task's human edge and how replaceable it is decide the move: defend, upgrade, watch, or pivot.*

Figure 12.1 *The Exposure-Advantage Test: two questions, replaceability and human edge, that route each task to a response.*

The stronghold, where the edge is strong and the task is hard to replace, is the safe ground: defend it and deepen it. Upgrade, where the edge is real but the task is replaceable, calls for handing the routine part to AI and concentrating on the judgment the machine cannot supply. Watch, hard to replace but carrying little edge, is stable for now and worth strengthening. And the move-ground response, easy to replace and low in edge, is where a pivot or a reinvention belongs. Most roles are a mix, and the exercise is to see which response holds the most weight.

A worked walk makes the test less abstract. Take a marketing role and run its tasks through it. Owning the brand's voice and the relationship with the biggest client: strong edge, hard to replace, a stronghold. Writing campaign copy and first-draft strategy: real edge, but increasingly replaceable, an upgrade. Pulling the weekly performance report: little edge and easy to replace, time to move ground. Managing the approval process: little edge, but tangled enough in people and politics to be hard to replace for now, one to watch. One role, spread across all four responses, and the plan falls out of the picture: defend the first, upgrade the second, hand off or move on from the third, and keep an eye on the fourth.

Upgrade: Stay and Rise

Upgrading is the most common response and the least disruptive, and it fits the many roles that are transforming rather than disappearing. The move is to add AI fluency, let the tools take the automatable part, and climb the judgment gap from Part Two. The role keeps its name and changes its hours. For most people, the best first step is not to flee a role but to upgrade it, because the role still carries real human edge and only the routine layer underneath it is being competed away.

The shape of an upgrade is concrete. A financial analyst stops hand-building the model the tool now assembles and spends the reclaimed hours on what the numbers mean for the decision at hand.

A teacher lets a model draft the first version of materials and redirects the saved time toward the part no model can do, the actual teaching of actual students. In each case the title is unchanged and the centre of gravity has moved, from producing the output to judging it and applying it. That migration, repeated across the tasks of a role, is what upgrading looks like in practice.

Upgrading well is more than learning a tool. It means deliberately shifting time from the part a machine now does toward the part only a person can: framing the problem, judging the output, owning the decision, carrying the relationship. A person who upgrades is not running faster on the same treadmill. They are stepping off the part of the work that is flattening and onto the part that is rising, while keeping the role and the income that funds the move.

Pivot: Sideways to Higher Ground

A pivot fits when much of a role is fading but the underlying skills transfer to an adjacent, rising one. The translator who moves into localization strategy and high-stakes work, the print designer who moves into digital product design, the support lead who moves into customer success and AI workflow design: each reuses most of what they already have and points it at work that is growing. A pivot is a shorter leap than it looks, because the transferable core, the domain knowledge, the relationships, the judgment, travels with the person.

The art of a pivot is identifying the adjacent ground early, while there is still a choice of where to land. The same domain expertise that is losing value in one configuration is often exactly what makes a person credible in a neighbouring one. The goal is not to abandon a career but to redeploy it, one step over, onto ground that is rising rather than sinking.

Finding the adjacent ground is a practical exercise, not a leap of faith. A person can list what they actually know, the domain, the relationships, the judgment, the context, and then ask which nearby roles are hungry for exactly those things and are rising rather than fading. The translator's deep grasp of two cultures is precisely what high-stakes localization and cross-border strategy need. The bookkeeper's intimate knowledge of small-business cash flow is exactly what advisory work runs on. The adjacent role is usually hiding in plain sight, one honest inventory away, defined by the transferable core a person already owns.

Reinvent: The Larger Leap

Reinvention is the response when a role is structurally disappearing and the skills do not transfer to anything close by. It is rare, and it is real. Reinvention means a deliberate, larger change: a new domain, serious retraining, and the harder work of letting go of an old professional identity. It is the most demanding of the three responses, and the one most worth starting early, because it takes the most time and is most painful when forced.

Reinvention has real examples behind it, and they are rarely glamorous. A travel agent whose core booking work was hollowed out by software and platforms, and whose skills did not transfer cleanly, retrained over two years into a different field entirely while working the old job part-time. The move was hard, slow, and frightening, and it worked precisely because it was begun early and built gradually, with the old income cushioning the new learning. Reinvention is the rarest response for a reason: most roles are transforming rather than vanishing outright, and most people are better served by upgrading or pivoting. But for the minority whose ground is truly disappearing, a deliberate, early reinvention is far kinder than a forced, late one.

Reinvention is rarely a single jump. It is usually built quietly in parallel: learning a new field on the side, taking on small projects in the new direction, building a second income or a portfolio before the old role ends. Done early and gradually, it is a deliberate transition. Done late and suddenly, it is a crisis. The difference is almost entirely a matter of when a person starts.

Optionality: A Side Bet While Standing Still

Underneath all three responses sits a quieter strategy: building optionality before it is needed. A small side project in an adjacent field, a second skill developed on evenings and weekends, a modest independent income, a network kept warm beyond the current employer, each is a cheap option that costs little while things are stable and pays enormously if they are not. Optionality is not disloyalty to a current role; it is insurance against a future no one can predict. The person holding two or three live options meets disruption as an inconvenience to be managed, while the person holding a single path meets it as a catastrophe. The time to build options is precisely when none of them feels urgent.

Letting Go of the Old Identity

The hardest part of any of these moves is rarely the new skill. It is the old identity. A person who has been the best translator in the office, or the one who builds the model, has woven the role into their sense of self, and the grief of setting that down is real and worth naming plainly. The capability mindset from Part One is the antidote: a person is not their title but their ability to learn what is needed next. Holding identity loosely, as a capability rather than a label, is what makes upgrading, pivoting, and reinventing emotionally possible and not merely technically sensible. The people who move well are the ones who can let an old self-description go without feeling that they themselves are being erased.

Separating the role from the contribution beneath it makes the letting go easier. A person did not, deep down, want the title for its own sake; they wanted to help a business stay solvent, or to let two cultures understand each other. The title was the vehicle, not the destination, and when the vehicle changes the contribution can continue in a new form. Naming that deeper thing, the purpose the title was always only a means to, is often what turns a frightening forced ending into a deliberate next chapter.

Timing: Move From Strength, Not Desperation

Across all three responses, the single most important variable is timing. The best time to move is early, while still employed, still paid, and still holding the slack to experiment and fail without ruin. The worst time is after the role has collapsed, when the move is forced, the finances are tight, and the choices have narrowed to whatever is left. Moving from strength is a decision; moving from desperation is a scramble, and the same change is far harder under the second condition than the first.

Sequencing the move is mostly common sense applied early. Build the new skill while the old salary still funds the learning. Take on a small project in the new direction before betting everything on it. Keep the current role performing while the next one is quietly assembled underneath. The aim is an overlap, a bridge from one foothold to the next, rather than a leap across a gap with nothing below. A transition built as an overlap rarely feels like a crisis, because at no point is a person standing on nothing.

There is a quieter advantage to moving early, too. The person who moves first has the pick of the adjacent ground before it crowds, and the time to learn before the learning is urgent. The heuristic is short. If most of the role still carries human edge and is transforming, upgrade. If the core is fading but the skills travel, pivot. If little survives and nothing transfers, reinvent. And whichever it is, begin while there is slack, and begin small. None of this requires certainty about the timeline. It requires honesty about exposure and the willingness to move before being made to. Knowing when disruption arrives and how to respond is most of the battle, but it leaves a question of place: which functions and industries get hit first, and where the new ground is forming. That is the territory of Part Four.

IN PRACTICE

A bookkeeper saw the writing on the wall as software began automating the data entry, reconciliation, and routine reporting that filled her days. Run through the test, most of her role fell where she least wanted to admit: easy to replace, low in human edge. Upgrading alone would not save a role that was mostly automatable in the first place.

But her skills transferred. She understood her clients' businesses, their cash worries, and the decisions that kept them up at night, and that understanding was rising in value at exactly the rate the data entry was falling. She pivoted, deliberately and early, from bookkeeping into advisory work, helping small-business owners read what the numbers meant and decide what to do next. She let the software do the part it did well and sold the judgment it could not, reusing almost everything she already knew. Above all she moved while the old work still paid the bills, which was the single thing that made the pivot a choice instead of a crisis.

IN SHORT

- There are three responses to disruption, not one: upgrade, pivot, and reinvent, matched to exposure and edge.
- The Exposure-Advantage Test weighs how replaceable a task is against the human edge it carries, and routes each task to a response.
- Upgrade (stay and add AI) fits transforming roles and is the most common best first move.
- Pivot (sideways to a rising adjacent role) fits when the core fades but skills transfer; reinvent (a larger leap) fits when little survives and nothing transfers.
- Timing decides everything: move from strength, early, while there is slack, not from desperation after the role collapses.

ASK YOURSELF

1 Run through the test, where do the main tasks of a role land: stronghold, upgrade, watch, or move ground?

2 If the honest answer is upgrade, what is the first AI fluency to build and the first task to hand over?

3 If it is pivot, which adjacent rising role would reuse the most of what is already known?

4 What would moving from strength look like, and what is the real cost of waiting until the move is forced?

PART FOUR

WHERE

Where AI Disruption Will Hit First

Disruption is not spread evenly: it arrives first where the work is most exposed and the friction lowest, and it builds new ground in the overlap between human and machine.

CHAPTER THIRTEEN
Disruption by Function

A natural question follows from the timeline and the signals: not only when, but where. Disruption does not arrive evenly across the economy. It lands first where the work is most exposed, and the clearest way to see the pattern is to look function by function, at the kind of work a person actually does, rather than by job title or industry alone.

Looking at functions rather than whole jobs is not only more accurate, it is calmer. "Will my job disappear" is an overwhelming, all-or-nothing question that invites either panic or denial. "Which of the functions in my job are exposed, and which are protected" is a question a person can actually answer and act on. The geography in this part is meant to be used that way: as a set of specific, answerable questions rather than a single alarming one.

Function, Not Job Title

A job title is a bundle of functions, and the bundle is what makes "will my job go" the wrong question. A marketing manager does some content creation, some analysis, some strategy, and some relationship management, and each of those functions sits on a different schedule. The useful exercise is to unbundle a role into its functions and ask, of each one, how exposed it is. Disruption happens to functions and tasks, and people feel it through whatever bundle of functions their particular title happens to contain.

The Pattern That Repeats

Across every function, the same fault line from Part Two reappears. The tasks that are routine, predictable, high-volume, and reducible to a pattern are the ones AI absorbs first. The tasks that demand judgment under uncertainty, trust, relationship, accountability, physical presence, or genuine novelty are the ones that stay human longest. Knowing this, a person can roughly predict what will happen inside any function before looking at the specifics: the templated middle hollows out, and the work migrates toward the judgment-heavy top and the relationship-heavy edges.

This is why the walk through the functions that follows is less a set of separate forecasts than a single prediction applied repeatedly. The details differ, but the shape is constant. In each function, ask which tasks are template-driven and which turn on judgment, and the exposed and protected parts sort themselves out.

Consider how it plays out in a single example. A loan officer's role contains data gathering, standardized assessment, document preparation, judgment calls on borderline cases, and the relationship with the borrower. The first three are template-driven and exposed; the last two turn on judgment and trust and are protected. The role neither vanishes nor survives as a whole. It is reweighted, losing mass on the exposed side and gaining it on the protected side, and the person who sees that early can lean into the protected part on purpose.

Functions Reshaping Fastest

Some functions are feeling it first, because so much of their work is digital, language-based, and pattern-rich.

Customer support. First-line support is among the most exposed functions of all, because a large share of it is answering common questions from a knowable body of information. Tools handle routine tickets, draft responses, and surface answers instantly. What remains human is the difficult, emotional, or novel case: the angry customer, the genuine exception, the moment when judgment and empathy matter more than the answer.

Marketing and content. First-draft copy, variations, basic creative, and routine campaign production are heavily exposed, because they are language and image generation at volume. What remains is strategy, brand judgment, taste, and the relationships that decide what is worth making in the first place.

Software and IT. Boilerplate code, documentation, first-pass debugging, and routine configuration are increasingly tool-assisted. What remains is architecture, judgment about trade-offs, understanding the messy real-world problem, and owning whether the system actually works. The junior who only typed known patterns is more exposed than the engineer who decides what to build and why.

What these three functions share is instructive. In each, the exposed part is the production of a first draft from a known pattern, and the protected part is the judgment about what to make and whether it is any good. That division, draft versus judgment, is the single most reliable guide to where a function is heading, and it recurs in every function that follows.

Figure 13.1 *Disruption by Function: the routine layer is exposed first, the judgment layer last.*

Functions Reshaping Steadily

Other functions are being reshaped at a steadier pace, often gated by regulation, risk, and the need for accountability.

The thread connecting these is accountability. In finance, HR, and law, someone must be answerable for the outcome to a regulator, a court, a board, or a person whose livelihood is affected. A tool can draft and analyse, but it cannot be accountable, and so these functions keep a human firmly in the loop at the points where responsibility lives. The routine production around those points is exposed; the accountable judgment at their centre is not.

Finance and accounting. Reconciliation, routine reporting, data entry, and first-pass analysis are highly automatable. What remains is judgment about what the numbers mean, the decisions they inform, and the accountability a regulator or a board demands of a named human being.

HR and learning. Screening, scheduling, and the drafting of materials are exposed. What remains is the human judgment in hiring, the handling of conflict and culture, and the coaching relationship that no tool can hold.

Legal. Document review, legal research, and first-draft contracts are being absorbed quickly, because much legal work is pattern-matching against precedent. What remains is judgment in genuinely novel situations, advocacy, negotiation, and the accountability of advising a client whose stakes are real.

Functions Reshaping More Slowly

A few functions are moving more slowly, not because they touch no exposed tasks but because their centre of gravity sits on the human side of the line.

High-end consulting. The research, synthesis, and deck production that fill junior consulting hours are exposed, which compresses the bottom of the pyramid. But the senior work, framing the real problem, navigating client politics, and carrying the judgment a board will act on, is far harder to automate, and may even rise in value as the routine layer cheapens.

Education. Content generation and some assessment support are exposed, and tools will change how material is made and delivered. But the core of teaching, the relationship, the motivation, the reading of a particular student in a particular moment, is deeply human, and the function as a whole is reshaped more than it is replaced.

The Squeeze on Entry-Level Work

One pattern cuts across all of these functions and deserves naming on its own: the work most exposed is often the work juniors have always done. The first-draft copy, the basic code, the document review, the routine analysis, the first-line ticket, these were the rungs by which people entered a profession and learned it. As tools absorb that rung, the bottom of the career ladder thins, and the path from novice to expert grows harder to climb.

This has two consequences worth holding together. For people early in a career, it means the old apprenticeship of doing routine work for years is shrinking, and the way in now runs through pairing with the tools and reaching for judgment sooner. For organizations, it raises a question they have barely begun to answer: if juniors no longer cut their teeth on the routine work, where will the next generation of seniors come from? The hollowing of the middle is not only a present disruption; it is a quiet problem stored up for the future.

Reading a Function Honestly

The practical takeaway is the same in every function, which is oddly reassuring. Inside whatever function a person works, the routine, templated layer is the exposed one, and the judgment, relationship, and accountability layer is the protected one. The move is identical regardless of field: hand the exposed layer to the tools, and climb deliberately toward the part of the function that turns on judgment. A function may be reshaping fast or slow, but the direction of safety within it always points the same way.

There is a subtler reading worth doing, too. Within a function, it is worth asking not only which tasks are exposed, but which of the protected tasks a person is actually good at and positioned to grow into. Knowing that judgment and relationship are protected is not enough; the question is whether a particular person is building real strength there, or merely hoping the protected layer will shelter them while they keep doing the exposed work. Protection is a property of tasks, not of people, and it shelters only those who move onto the protected ground deliberately.

Knowing which functions are most exposed is half of the geography. The other half is industry, because the very same function can be disrupted at very different speeds depending on the industry it sits in. A marketing function inside a fast-moving technology company and the identical function inside a heavily regulated bank are on different clocks, and that difference is the subject of the next chapter.

IN PRACTICE

A customer support team lead watched AI tools absorb the routine half of her team's work within a year: password resets, order status, the same forty questions answered ten thousand times over. The volume that once justified a large team was now handled instantly, and the pressure to shrink the team was immediate and obvious.

Rather than defend the headcount or deny the change, she unbundled the function honestly. The routine tickets were going, and arguing about it would not bring them back. But the difficult cases, the furious customer, the genuine exception, the problem no script covered, were now a larger share of the work, and they needed judgment, empathy, and authority the tools did not have. She rebuilt the team around those cases, moved her best people up into handling complexity and coaching the tools, and turned a function being hollowed out into one being elevated. The same disruption that threatened the team became the argument for redesigning it.

IN SHORT

- Disruption lands on functions and tasks, not tidy job titles; the useful move is to unbundle a role into its functions.

- In every function the same split repeats: routine, templated tasks are exposed, while judgment, relationship, and accountability stay human longest.
- Functions reshaping fastest are the most digital and language-rich: support, marketing and content, software and IT.
- Finance, HR, and legal reshape steadily, often gated by accountability and risk; high-end consulting and education move more slowly.
- Within any function the direction of safety is the same: hand off the routine layer and climb toward the judgment-heavy core.

ASK YOURSELF

1. Unbundled into its functions, which parts of a role are most exposed and which are most protected?
2. Within a function, which tasks are template-driven and which turn on judgment, relationship, or accountability?
3. Is a role currently weighted toward the exposed layer of its function or the protected one?
4. What would climbing toward the judgment-heavy core of a function actually involve this year?

CHAPTER FOURTEEN

Disruption by Industry

The same function can be disrupted at very different speeds depending on where it sits, which is why industry is the second axis of the geography. A capable professional in a slow industry can stay comfortable for years while the identical skills are being competed away rapidly one industry over. Reading the industry clock matters as much as reading the function.

The reason is straightforward. A tool's capability is roughly the same everywhere, but its deployment is not. The same model that can draft a contract is allowed to do so freely in one setting and hedged with review, approval, and liability in another. So two people doing identical work can face very different timelines purely because of the industry they sit in and the friction that industry carries. Capability sets what is possible; industry sets how soon it becomes real.

Two Forces Set the Pace

Two forces, multiplied together, set how fast an industry feels AI. The first is exposure: how much of the industry's core work is digital, cognitive, and pattern-rich, the kind of work tools do well. The second is adoption friction: how much regulation, risk, liability, trust, and structural inertia slow the industry's ability to actually deploy the tools, however capable they are. A highly exposed industry with low friction moves fast; a highly exposed industry with high friction moves slowly, despite the capability being fully present.

This is why capability alone does not predict disruption. The technology may be ready to transform medicine or law tomorrow, but a hospital or a court cannot, and should not, adopt as fast as a software startup. The friction is often there for good reasons: safety, accountability, due process. It buys time. What it does not do is change the destination.

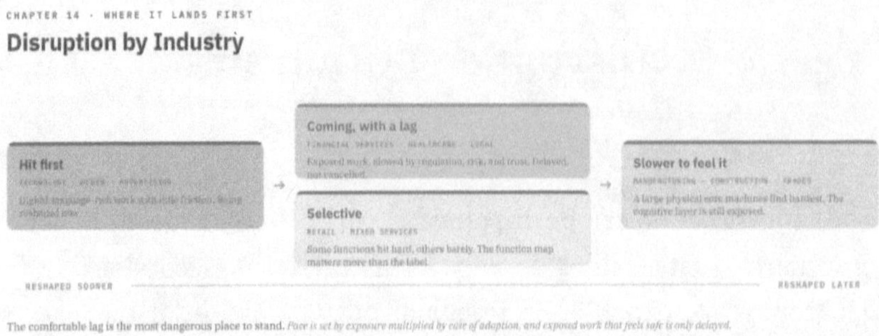

Figure 14.1 *Disruption by Industry: which industries are reshaped first, set by exposure multiplied by ease of adoption.*

Hit First: High Exposure, Low Friction

Industries that combine high exposure with low friction are feeling it first. Technology and software, media and publishing, advertising and marketing services, and digital-first businesses of every kind live in exactly the medium AI is strongest in: language, code, images, and data. They also face little regulatory friction and a culture that rewards fast adoption. In these industries the disruption is not a forecast but a present reality, reshaping roles and team sizes already.

For people in these industries, the lesson is not despair but speed. The disruption is visible, which is itself a kind of gift, because it removes the option of pretending. The professionals who thrive here are the ones who treat the obviousness of the change as permission to move now, upgrading and repositioning while the industry is still sorting itself out, rather than waiting for a stability that a fast, low-friction industry will never provide.

Coming, With a Lag

Other industries are just as exposed but slowed by friction. Financial services, healthcare and pharmaceuticals, and legal services all run on exactly the cognitive, document-heavy, pattern-rich work AI does well, which makes them highly exposed. But heavy regulation, real liability, and the need for trust and accountability slow the pace of adoption, sometimes by years.

The lag is real, and it is a trap if it is misread. People in these industries can point, accurately, to all the reasons their work cannot simply be handed to a machine tomorrow, and then conclude, inaccurately, that it never will be. The friction delays the disruption; it does not cancel it. The wise read the lag as a gift of time to prepare; the complacent read it as proof of safety, and waste it.

History gives the complacent reading little support. The same confident case, that the work is too regulated, too sensitive, or too human to automate, was made in industry after industry just before the automation arrived, usually not as a sudden replacement but as a slow erosion of the tasks around the edges. Regulation and trust do raise the cost of moving fast, and they genuinely buy time, but they rarely hold the line forever, because the commercial pressure to adopt only builds while the friction slowly gives way. The industries that feel safest today are often the ones storing up the sharpest adjustment for later, precisely because the lag let them avoid preparing.

Geography Runs Down to the Firm

Industry is not the finest grain of the map. Within any industry, individual firms move at very different speeds, and the specific employer often matters more than the sector. One bank builds an AI function and rewires its workflows while another, down the street, bans the tools and waits. Two underwriters with the same title, the same skills, and the same industry can be on entirely different clocks because of nothing more than their employer's appetite for change.

This means a person's real exposure is set by three nested layers: the function they perform, the industry they work in, and the particular firm that employs them. A protected function in a slow industry at a cautious firm is about as sheltered as the current landscape allows. An exposed function in a fast industry at an aggressive firm is the opposite, and feels the change first and hardest. An exposed function in a fast industry at an aggressive adopter is the opposite. Most people sit somewhere in between, and locating oneself honestly across all three layers is more useful than any single headline about the economy.

The practical move is to read all three layers honestly, rather than taking comfort from the most favourable one. A person in an exposed function can still be relatively safe at a slow firm in a slow industry, and a person in a protected function can be surprisingly exposed at an aggressive firm racing to adopt. The mistake is to read only the layer that reassures: the slow industry, the cautious employer, the human-sounding job title. The honest reading looks at the fastest-moving of the three, because that is the one that sets the real clock.

None of this argues for panic in the slower industries, which would be its own mistake. It argues for using the time the lag provides instead of spending it. The professional in a sheltered position holds the rarest thing in a disruption, which is room to prepare without immediate pressure, and the choice that matters is whether that room is used to build fluency and reposition early, or merely to enjoy a postponement that ends without warning. The lag is an opportunity or a trap depending entirely on what is done with it.

Selective, and Slower to Feel It

Some industries are mixed, hit hard in some functions and barely touched in others. Retail sees heavy exposure in marketing, support, and supply-chain analytics, while the physical, in-store, and logistics work is far less exposed. In mixed industries the function map from the previous chapter matters more than the industry label, because the average hides the variance.

Industries built on physical work feel the cognitive wave last and least. Manufacturing, construction, skilled trades, and hands-on services have a large physical core that, by Moravec's paradox from Part Two, is exactly what machines find hardest. Their cognitive and administrative layers, scheduling, design, paperwork, are exposed, but the core of the work resists. This does not make them immune, and robotics will change the picture over a longer horizon, but on the timeline that matters for current careers, these industries move slowly.

It is worth being precise about what slowly means, though. The administrative and design layers around physical work are exposed even where the physical core is not, so even slow industries feel the wave at their edges. A construction firm's estimating, scheduling, and paperwork can be reshaped long before anything changes on the site itself. Slow is not the same as untouched, and the exposed edges of a physical industry are still worth watching closely.

Using the Map

The map is meant to be stood on, not merely admired. A person can locate themselves with three questions. Is the function I perform exposed or protected? Is the industry I work in hit-first, lagging, mixed, or slow? And is my particular employer an eager adopter or a reluctant one? The three answers together give a far sharper read on personal timing than any forecast about AI in general, and, unlike a forecast, they can be acted on directly, because each of the three is something a person can actually see and, to some degree, choose.

Why the Lag Is Dangerous

The deepest risk in this whole map is not being in a fast industry. People in fast industries can see the wave and have no choice but to respond. The deeper risk is the comfortable lag of a slow or high-friction industry, where the disruption is coming but not yet visible, and where every day of delay feels validated by the fact that nothing has happened yet. The lag is the most dangerous place to stand precisely because it feels the safest.

The remedy is to invert the instinct. Instead of taking the absence of visible disruption as reassurance, a person in a lagging industry can treat it as a countdown already running, and ask what they would want to have built by the time the lag ends. The discomfort of preparing for a threat that has not yet materialized is small. The discomfort of being unprepared when it does is not. In a lag, the only mistake that is hard to recover from is mistaking borrowed time for safe ground.

Together, function and industry locate where the ground is least stable. But a map of where work is being lost is only half a map. The same forces that are remaking these functions and industries are also creating new work, and the final chapter of this part is about where that new ground is forming.

IN PRACTICE

An insurance underwriter worked in an industry everyone agreed was slow: heavily regulated, risk-averse, and bound by accountability requirements that no tool could simply absorb. Her colleagues took comfort in the friction, certain that underwriting judgment would stay human for a long time, and used that certainty as a reason to change nothing.

She read the same friction differently, as a countdown rather than a guarantee. The core of her work, the routine risk assessment against known patterns, was exactly what the tools were getting good at, and the regulation slowing adoption was a delay, not a reprieve. She spent the borrowed time deliberately: learning the tools, moving her focus toward the complex and novel cases where judgment genuinely mattered, and positioning herself as the person who could combine the models' speed with the accountability the regulator required. When adoption finally reached her firm, the lag her colleagues had treated as safety had been, for her, a head start.

IN SHORT

- The same function is disrupted at different speeds in different industries; industry is the second axis of the geography.
- Two forces set the pace: exposure (how digital and cognitive the core work is) and adoption friction (regulation, risk, trust, inertia).
- High exposure with low friction is hit first: technology, media, advertising, and digital-first businesses.

- High exposure with high friction comes with a lag: financial services, healthcare, and legal, where disruption is delayed, not cancelled.
- Physical industries feel the cognitive wave last; the most dangerous place to stand is the comfortable lag that feels safe but is not.

ASK YOURSELF

1. How exposed is the core work of a given industry, and how much friction slows its adoption?
2. Is an industry hit-first, lagging, mixed, or slow, and what does that imply about timing?
3. Where a lag exists, is it being used to prepare, or mistaken for permanent safety?
4. Could the same skills be facing a faster clock in a neighbouring industry?

CHAPTER FIFTEEN

Where New Opportunities Will Be Created

Every wave of disruption is also a wave of creation, and an account of where work is being lost would be dishonest if it stopped there. The harder and more useful question is where the new work is forming, and there is a test that separates the durable new opportunities from the passing ones.

This matters because the temptation, faced with a map of disruption, is to read it only defensively, as a list of threats to avoid. But the same forces that hollow out old work are building new work, and a person who plays only defense will miss the more interesting half of the picture. The aim of this chapter is not reassurance that everything will be fine, which no one can honestly promise, but a method for finding the ground that is rising rather than only fleeing the ground that is sinking.

Disruption Creates as It Destroys

History is consistent on one point: technologies that destroy categories of work also create new ones, and the new categories are usually hard to see in advance. The roles the web created were not obvious before the web, and the same will be true here. This is genuine grounds for optimism, with one honest caveat: the new work rarely lands in the same place or at the same time as the old, so seeing where it forms early is itself an advantage.

The caveat deserves weight, because glib optimism does real harm. "Technology always creates more jobs than it destroys" may even be true over decades, and it is no comfort at all to a specific person in a specific year whose specific role has gone. The honest position holds both halves: new work is genuinely coming, and the transition to it is genuinely hard, and pretending otherwise in either direction helps no one. The right response to that honesty is not to wait for the new jobs to arrive, but to move toward where they are already forming.

The Complementarity Test

The test for durable new work is complementarity. The best new roles sit not where AI is strong alone, because that work gets fully automated and needs no human, and not where humans work entirely without AI, because that work is simply unchanged, but in the overlap, where humans and AI are each strongest and the value comes from combining them. Work that needs both a human's judgment and a machine's scale, and would be worse with either one missing, is work that lasts.

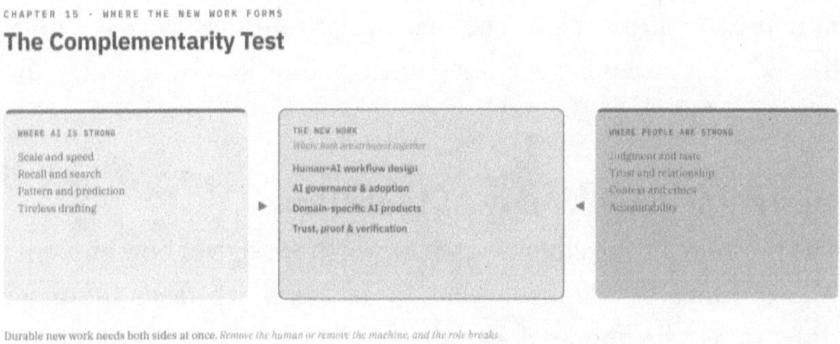

Figure 15.1 *The Complementarity Test: the best new work sits where both are strongest together.*

The test is practical. Faced with any emerging role, ask: does this depend on a real human strength, judgment, trust, taste, accountability, and on a real machine strength, scale, speed, recall, pattern, such that removing either would break it? If the answer is yes, it sits in the complementary zone, and it is the kind of ground worth moving toward. If it leans entirely on one side, it is either a target for automation or unchanged old work.

Why Complementary Work Lasts

Complementary work is durable for a structural reason, not a sentimental one. Work that depends only on the machine's strength has an obvious failure mode: as the machine improves, the human in the loop becomes friction to be removed, and the role is automated away. Work that depends only on human strength is stable but not new, and it does not grow simply because AI arrived. Complementary work is different: as the machine gets better, the human half does not shrink, it gains leverage, because a more capable tool makes the judgment that directs it more valuable, not less. The better the engine, the more the steering matters.

That principle reframes the whole anxiety about being automated. The fear assumes a fixed amount of work, shrinking as machines take pieces of it. Complementarity describes the opposite dynamic in the right places: a growing amount of work, as more capable tools open up tasks that were not worth doing before and create fresh demand for the judgment to direct them. The person positioned in the overlap is not defending a shrinking territory but standing where new territory is being made.

Designing the Human-AI Workflow

The most broadly useful new category is the design of how humans and AI work together. Someone has to decide which tasks the machine does, which the human does, where the handoffs are, how the output is checked, and who is accountable when it matters. This is a genuinely new discipline, and it sits squarely in the complementary zone. It shows up as AI-enabled consulting and advisory, where the value is not the raw analysis a tool can now do, but the judgment to design the system and interpret what it produces.

This is less exotic than it sounds. Every team adopting these tools quietly faces a hundred small design questions, and most answer them by accident. The person who answers them on purpose, who maps the work, places the tool where it helps, guards the points where a mistake would be costly, and keeps a human owning the result, is doing the new job whether or not it has a name yet. The discipline is portable across domains, because the questions are the same wherever humans and machines share the work.

The same is true of advisory work built on top of these tools. Clients no longer need to pay for the analysis a model can now produce cheaply, but they will pay, more than before, for someone who can decide which questions are worth asking, judge whether the machine's answers can be trusted, and stand behind the recommendation. The raw output has been commoditised; the judgment wrapped around it has become the product.

Owning the result is the part that does not transfer to the machine. A client, a patient, a court, or a board wants a person to stand behind a judgment, to be reachable when it goes wrong, and to carry the responsibility that software cannot hold. As routine production gets cheaper, that willingness to be accountable grows more valuable, not less, and it is available to anyone prepared to take it on. Accountability is a choice as much as a skill, and it is one of the surest paths into the complementary zone.

Governing the Machines

As organizations adopt AI, a whole field opens around doing it responsibly. AI governance, ethics, safety, compliance, and the practical work of training people and managing adoption are all growing, and all complementary by nature: they require human judgment about values and risk applied to machine capability. Helping an organization adopt AI well, safely, and in line with its obligations is work that exists only because the machines do, and that only humans can do.

Governance work also tends to be durable because it grows with adoption rather than being consumed by it. The more capable and widespread the tools become, the more an organization needs people who can set the rules, watch the edges, and answer for the results. It is one of the clearer cases where the machine's advance increases the demand for a particular kind of human judgment instead of erasing it, which is precisely the signature of complementary work.

Building Domain-Specific AI

General tools create demand for people who can point them at specific domains. The person who understands a particular field deeply, medicine, law, logistics, education, and can shape AI tools to serve it well is in a strong position, because the scarce ingredient is not the model but the domain judgment that makes it useful and safe in context. Domain depth plus AI fluency is one of the most durable combinations the new landscape rewards.

The pattern is visible already. A radiologist who helps shape an imaging tool, a logistics manager who tunes a routing system, a teacher who guides an educational tool toward how students actually learn, each turns deep domain knowledge into the thing that makes a general tool genuinely useful in a specific world. The model is close to a commodity; the domain judgment that aims it is not.

This is encouraging news for experienced people who fear their field is being automated. The very domain depth that took years to build, and that can feel stranded when the routine tasks around it are absorbed, is the scarce complement that makes the tools work. The expertise is not obsolete; it is the ingredient in shortest supply. The task is to recombine it with fluency in the tools rather than to abandon it.

There is a generational point hidden here as well. Younger workers often have the fluency but not yet the domain depth; experienced workers often have the depth but not yet the fluency. Neither half is sufficient alone, and the people who pair the two, whether an experienced person learning the tools or a fluent one going deep in a domain, reach the complementary ground first. Mentorship in both directions, depth taught one way and fluency the other, may be one of the most valuable exchanges a team can run.

Guarding Trust

As generation becomes cheap and convincing, proof becomes precious. Verification, provenance, authentication, and deepfake detection, the whole apparatus of establishing what is real and who is accountable for it, grows in value exactly as fakery gets easier. This is a clear complementary frontier: machines generate at scale, and humans, aided by tools, must verify, attribute, and vouch.

These four areas, workflow design, governance, domain-specific products, and trust, are examples rather than a complete list, and new ones will keep appearing. What they share is the structure the test describes: each needs a human and a machine together, and would collapse if either were removed. That shared structure is more useful to remember than the specific list, because the list will change while the structure will not. When a new opportunity appears, the question is always the same one: does it live in the overlap?

It is worth saying plainly that none of this guarantees a soft landing for everyone. Some people will find the move to complementary work natural, others difficult, and the transition will be easier for those with more time, resources, and support. The Complementarity Test is a compass, not a promise. What it offers is direction: a reliable way to tell ground that is forming from ground that is washing away, so that effort and learning can be pointed somewhere they will still matter in five years.

It also helps to notice that the complementary zone is not a single far-off destination but a direction that can be travelled from anywhere. A nurse, an accountant, a teacher, a logistics planner: each has a version of the overlap specific to their field, reachable from where they already stand. The test does not point everyone toward the same handful of fashionable roles. It points each person toward the place, in their own domain, where their particular judgment and the machine's particular power combine into something neither could do alone.

Positioning for the New Work

The mistake is to chase a specific new job title, which may not exist yet, or may be named something else by the time it matters. The better move is to build the complementary stance the new work rewards: deep domain judgment, real AI fluency, and the ability to design and own the combination. These are general bets that pay off across whichever specific roles emerge. The new ground is reached not by predicting the exact destination, but by walking, deliberately, toward the overlap.

Concretely, that walk has a shape. It usually starts with becoming genuinely fluent with the tools in one's own domain, not as a dabbler but as someone who knows their edges. It continues by taking on the work others avoid, the messy intersection of the human and the machine, where the handoffs are unclear and the judgment is hard. And it compounds by becoming the person others turn to when they need both the tool used well and someone accountable for the result. None of these steps requires a new title or anyone's permission. They require only a deliberate lean toward the overlap, starting from wherever a person already stands.

None of this dissolves the genuine difficulty of the moment, and it is not meant to. What it offers is a place to point the effort. A person who knows that the durable new work lives in the overlap, and who has a compass for finding their own version of it, is in a fundamentally different position from one who only knows that something is changing and feels the ground move. The first can act; the second can only worry. This whole part has been about turning that worry into a map.

A final reassurance is in order. Walking toward the overlap does not mean abandoning everything familiar and starting from zero. For most people it means a series of small, deliberate reorientations: one new tool learned properly, one messy human-and-machine problem taken on, one reputation slowly built as the person who makes the combination work. The new ground is reached by accumulation, not by a single dramatic leap, and almost anyone can begin that accumulation from where they already stand.

This completes the geography. The earlier parts established why AI is different, what it can and cannot do, and when it lands, and this part has mapped where it hits first and where the new ground forms. What remains is the heart of the book: how to actually respond. That is the work of Part Five, where the practical method begins.

IN PRACTICE

A compliance officer had spent years on regulatory paperwork, much of which AI could increasingly draft and check. Seen narrowly, her role was exposed. Seen through the Complementarity Test, she was sitting on exactly the combination the new work rewarded: deep judgment about rules and risk, applied to a powerful new machine capability that organizations were adopting faster than they could govern.

She moved, deliberately, into AI governance, helping her organization adopt the tools responsibly, setting the policies for what the machines could and could not decide, and owning the accountability that no model can carry. The work existed only because the machines did, and it required exactly the human judgment a machine lacks, which is the definition of complementary work. She had not predicted the title, which barely existed when she started toward it. She had simply walked toward the overlap, where her judgment and the machine's capability were each strongest together, and found the new ground waiting for her there.

IN SHORT

- Disruption creates new work as it destroys old work; the new categories are usually hard to see in advance.
- The Complementarity Test: durable new work sits where humans and AI are each strongest together, not where either works alone.
- Major emerging areas include human-AI workflow design and AI-enabled advisory, and AI governance, ethics, and adoption.
- They also include domain-specific AI shaped by deep field expertise, and the trust work of verification, provenance, and deepfake detection.

- The way to position is not to chase a title but to build the complementary stance: domain judgment, AI fluency, and ownership of the combination.

ASK YOURSELF

1. Applied to an emerging role, does it depend on both a real human strength and a real machine strength, such that removing either would break it?
2. Where could existing domain depth combine with AI fluency to point at the complementary zone?
3. Which of the new areas, workflow design, governance, domain products, or trust, sits closest to current skills?
4. What is one deliberate step toward the overlap that could begin now, without waiting for the exact role to be named?

PART FIVE

HOW

How AI Actually Disrupts Careers and Businesses

Disruption is not a single event but a process: it climbs from task to identity, unbundles every role, reshapes the business around cost, and remakes how skill itself is built.

CHAPTER SIXTEEN

The Five Levels of AI Disruption

When people imagine AI disrupting their work, they usually picture a single moment: a tool arrives, a task disappears, a job is gone. The reality is less like a moment and more like a rising tide that climbs through five distinct levels, each one wider and deeper than the last. Seeing the levels clearly is what allows a person to respond to the disruption that is actually happening, rather than to the cartoon version of it.

The instinct to picture disruption as one event is natural but costly, because it leads people to prepare for the wrong thing. Bracing for a single dramatic moment, the day the job is abolished, they miss the gradual, multi-level reality already underway. The change does not usually arrive with an announcement. It arrives as a slow reweighting that, looked at level by level, is both easier to see and easier to act on than the imagined catastrophe.

Disruption Is Not One Event

Disruption operates at five levels: task, role, team, business model, and identity. They form a sequence, not because each strictly causes the next, but because the pressure that starts at the bottom tends to climb. A task is automated; the role built on that task shifts; the team built on that role restructures; the business model built on that team adapts; and somewhere in all of it, a person's sense of who they are professionally is called into question. Most people watch only the level they can see most easily, usually the first, and are caught off guard by the rest.

The five levels are worth holding in mind together because they explain a common and painful experience: doing everything right at one level and still being blindsided from another. A person can adapt their tasks beautifully and still have their team dissolved; a team can perform superbly and still be undone when the business model beneath it changes. Watching only one level is how capable people get surprised. The map is a way of keeping all five in view at once, so the surprise arrives less often.

Level One: The Task

The first level is the task, and it is where almost everyone first feels the change. A single, definable piece of work, drafting a summary, writing a routine function, answering a common query, is suddenly something a tool can do. This level is concrete and, in a sense, the least alarming, because a task is a small thing and handing it over can feel like relief. The mistake is to assume the disruption stops here. A task absorbed is rarely the end of the story; it is the first sign that the story has begun.

Level Two: The Role

When enough tasks within a job are absorbed, the role itself begins to change. Its centre of gravity moves: the work that defined it shrinks, and what remains is a different mix, usually weighted toward judgment, coordination, and the things a tool cannot do. The job may keep its title while quietly becoming a different job. This is the level at which a changing set of tasks becomes a changing role, and where the question shifts from what a person does to what the role is now actually for.

Level Three: The Team

Roles do not change in isolation. When many roles on a team are reshaped at once, the team restructures. The mix of skills changes, the number of people needed changes, and the workflows that connected them are redrawn. A team that needed ten people doing a certain blend of work may need six doing a different blend. At this level the disruption stops being personal and becomes organizational, and an individual's fate becomes bound up with decisions made above their head.

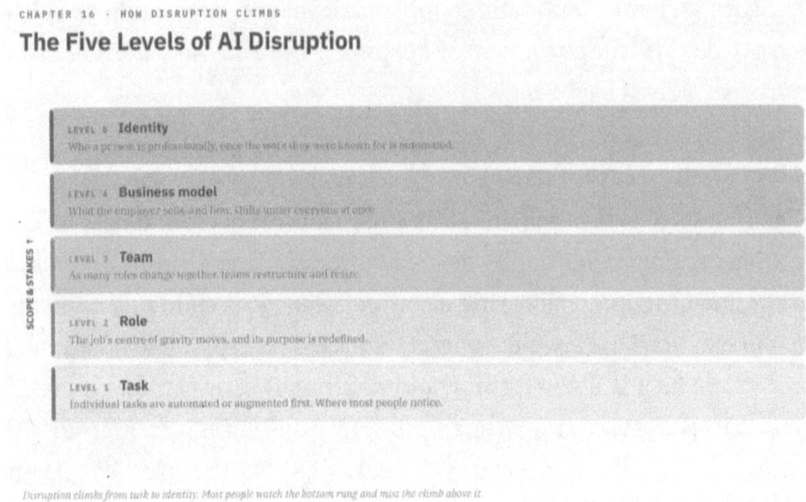

Figure 16.1 *The Five Levels of AI Disruption: the pressure climbs from task to identity.*

Level Four: The Business Model

Higher still, AI changes what a business sells and how it makes money. When the cost and speed of core work change dramatically, the things a company can profitably offer change with them, and sometimes the whole basis of the business shifts. A firm that sold hours may start selling outcomes; a service that depended on scarce expertise may find that expertise commoditized. At this level the ground moves under everyone in the organization at once, regardless of how well any individual has adapted their own role.

Level Five: Identity

The deepest level is identity, and it is where the real fear lives. When the work a person spent years mastering, the work that became part of who they are, is suddenly something a machine does, the question stops being practical and turns personal: who am I, if not the thing I was? This level is rarely discussed because it is uncomfortable, but it is often what makes the lower levels so hard to face honestly. A threat to a task is a problem; a threat to an identity feels like an erasure, and people will deny the first to avoid confronting the second.

The way through the identity level is not to pretend it does not exist, but to loosen the grip of the old self-description before it is pried loose by events. A person who has quietly decided that their worth lies in their ability to learn and contribute, rather than in one particular craft, has already done the hardest part. The identity question is answered best in advance, in calm, rather than in the panic of a role collapsing, and the people who have done that inner work are the ones who can act clearly when the lower levels start to move.

Responding at the Right Level

Seeing the five levels is useful because it shows where to act. Most people get stuck at one of two extremes. Some fixate on the first level, managing individual tasks, congratulating themselves for adopting a tool, and missing the role and team changes climbing up behind it. Others jump straight to the fifth, frozen by an identity crisis, and skip the levels where action is actually possible. The leverage is in the middle. Levels two, three, and four, the role, the team, and the business model, are where a person can still see the change coming and reposition on purpose.

And the identity question, level five, is best answered not by clinging to an old self-description but by the capability mindset from the earlier parts: a person is not a fixed role but a capacity to learn the next one. The levels that feel most threatening are usually best disarmed by working the levels below them. The next chapter goes down to the foundation, the task level, with a practical method for taking a role apart and deciding, task by task, what to hand over and what to keep.

IN PRACTICE

A litigation paralegal first felt the change at the task level, when a tool began handling the document review and first-draft discovery summaries that had filled her days. At first it felt like relief: the tedious work was lifting. She did not yet see that the relief was only the first level of something larger.

Within a year she watched it climb. Her role was redefined around exceptions and judgment rather than volume; the team shrank as fewer paralegals were needed for the same caseload; and the firm began rethinking how it priced work that no longer took the hours it once had. Somewhere in all of it came the personal question, the fifth level, of who she was if not the person who could out-work anyone on a document review. She answered it not by mourning the old role but by climbing toward the judgment the tools could not supply: the case strategy, the witness preparation, the read of a situation no model could make. She had seen the disruption climbing, and chosen to climb ahead of it.

IN SHORT

- AI disruption operates at five climbing levels: task, role, team, business model, and identity.
- It usually begins at the task level, where a tool absorbs a definable piece of work, then climbs as roles, teams, and models adjust.
- The identity level, where a person's professional self-image is threatened, is the deepest, and is often what makes the lower levels hard to face honestly.
- Most people get stuck managing the task level or frozen at the identity level, and miss the actionable middle.
- The leverage is at the role, team, and model levels, where change can be seen coming and met with deliberate repositioning.

ASK YOURSELF

1 At which of the five levels, task, role, team, business model, or identity, is disruption currently being felt most?

2 Is attention stuck on managing individual tasks while role or team changes climb unnoticed?

3 What would repositioning at the role or team level look like, before those changes are forced?

4 If the identity question feels threatening, what capability, rather than what title, could a professional self-image rest on instead?

CHAPTER SEVENTEEN

How Your Job Gets Unbundled

If disruption climbs from the task level upward, then the task level is where a person has the most control, and the most useful skill is the ability to take a job apart. A role that feels like a single, solid thing is in fact a bundle of separate tasks, each with its own exposure, and learning to unbundle it is the practical heart of responding well.

Every Job Is a Bundle of Tasks

No one is hired to do a job in the abstract. A job is a collection of tasks bundled together, historically, because it made sense for one person to do them all. A recruiter sources candidates, screens them, schedules interviews, coordinates feedback, manages offers, and advises hiring managers. Those are six different tasks with six different exposures, bundled under a single title. Disruption does not respect the bundle; it hits the tasks. So the analysis has to happen at the level of tasks, not titles.

The Unbundling Exercise

The exercise is simple to describe and revealing to do. List the actual tasks that fill a working week, honestly and specifically, not the tidy version from a job description but the real one. Then, for each task, ask two questions: what can a tool already do here, and what must a human own? The point is not to predict the distant future but to see the present clearly, because most people have never looked at their own work this way, and the picture is usually sharper than they expect.

The result is almost never all exposed or all safe. It is a mix: some tasks a tool can largely handle now, some it can assist with, and some that remain firmly human. That mix is the real map of a role, far more useful than any headline about whether the job, taken as a whole, is safe.

A worked example makes it concrete. An accountant might list: entering transactions, reconciling accounts, preparing standard statements, flagging anomalies, advising a client on a decision, and handling a tax authority's query. The first three are largely automatable now; flagging anomalies is shared work, where the tool surfaces and the human judges; and the last two, advising and representing, remain firmly human. One title, six tasks, four different verdicts. That distribution, not the job title, is what tells the accountant where their future actually lies.

The Delegation Test

Sorting the tasks needs a rule, and a good one has three parts. A task is a strong candidate to hand to AI when it is repeatable, low in judgment, and easy to verify. Repeatable means it follows a pattern rather than being a fresh problem each time. Low in judgment means little is lost if it is done in a standard way rather than with fine discretion. And easy to verify means a person can quickly tell whether the output is right.

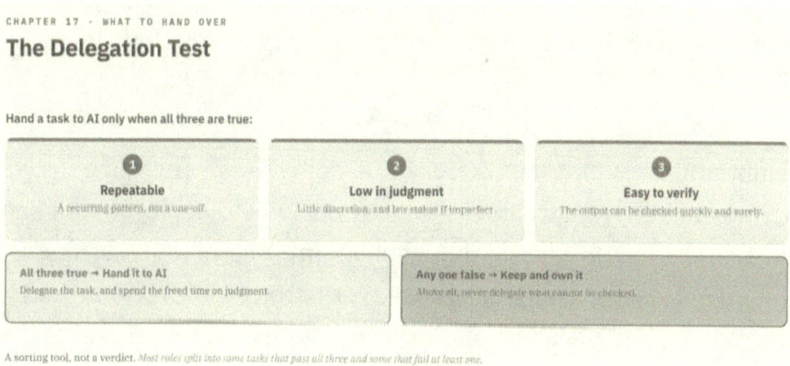

Figure 17.1 *The Delegation Test: hand over only what is repeatable, low in judgment, and easy to verify.*

The third criterion is the one most people neglect, and it is the most important. It is tempting to delegate the tasks a person understands least, precisely because they are tedious or hard. But handing over work that cannot be checked is how errors slip through invisibly. The safest tasks to delegate are the ones where a mistake would be caught at a glance. Where verification is hard, the human stays in the loop, not out of pride but out of prudence.

There is a second, quieter use of the test. It also reveals which skills a person most needs to keep sharp, namely the ones that do the verifying. A person who delegates a task but can no longer check the result has not saved effort; they have taken on risk. So the judgment required to verify the tool's output is itself a skill worth protecting, and sometimes the very reason to keep doing a little of the routine work by hand is to stay good enough at it to catch the machine when it is wrong.

What Humans Must Own

The Delegation Test, run in reverse, defines the protected core. The tasks that fail it, the ones that are novel, high in judgment, or hard to verify, are exactly the tasks a person should keep and deepen. These tend to be the tasks that carry stakes and accountability: the borderline decision, the difficult conversation, the call that cannot be standardized, the work where being wrong is expensive and being right requires understanding the whole situation. This is the human side of the bundle, and it is where a career's security increasingly lives.

Finding the New Value Zone

Unbundling is not an exercise in doing less. The time freed by delegating the repeatable tasks is meant to be redeployed, not simply lost, and where it goes is the whole point. The new value zone is the judgment-heavy, complementary work from the previous part: the tasks that combine a person's expertise with the tool's power and only grow more valuable as the tools improve. A role is not just stripped down; it is re-concentrated around the work that matters most, with the routine handed off to make room.

Done well, this is an upgrade rather than a loss. The person delegates the parts of the job a machine does better, reclaims the hours, and pours them into the parts a machine cannot touch. The job gets smaller in volume and larger in value, which is precisely the trade a person wants to be making before they are forced into it.

Running the Sort Again

Because the boundary keeps moving as tools improve, the unbundling is not a one-time exercise but a periodic one. A task that needed a human last year may pass the Delegation Test this year, and a person who re-runs the sort every so often stays ahead of the line rather than behind it. The habit matters more than any single result: the people who fare best are not those who guessed the boundary correctly once, but those who keep checking where it has moved.

Unbundling is how an individual responds to disruption at the task level. Organizations run exactly the same exercise on a larger scale, and with a different motive. Where a person unbundles a role to protect and re-concentrate their value, a business unbundles its work to reduce its cost, and understanding how it does so is the subject of the next chapter.

IN PRACTICE

A product designer took the unbundling exercise seriously and listed every task in a typical week: user research, wireframing, visual design, writing interface copy, building prototypes, presenting to stakeholders, and arguing for the user in the room. Run through the Delegation Test, the picture was clear. Generating wireframe variations and first-draft copy was repeatable, low in judgment, and easy to verify, ideal to hand over.

The rest failed the test in instructive ways. Understanding what users actually needed was neither repeatable nor easy to verify; deciding which design was right turned on judgment a tool could not supply; and advocating for the user against business pressure was pure accountability. So she delegated the production and poured the reclaimed hours into the research and judgment that defined good design. Her output of polished screens went up, and the value of her role shifted decisively toward the parts a tool could not touch. She had not been diminished by the tools; she had been re-concentrated by them.

IN SHORT

- Every job is a bundle of separate tasks, each with its own exposure; disruption hits tasks, so the analysis must happen at the task level.
- The unbundling exercise lists the real tasks of a week and asks, of each, what a tool can do and what a human must own.
- The Delegation Test hands a task to AI only when it is repeatable, low in judgment, and easy to verify.
- The hardest criterion is verification: work that cannot be checked should not be delegated, however tedious it is.
- The time freed by delegating routine tasks is meant to be redeployed into judgment-heavy, complementary work, re-concentrating a role around what matters.

ASK YOURSELF

1 Listed honestly, what are the actual tasks of a typical week, beyond the tidy job description?

2 Run through the Delegation Test, which tasks are repeatable, low in judgment, and easy enough to verify to hand over?

3 Which tasks fail the test, especially on verification, and therefore define the protected core?

4 Where could the hours freed by delegating be redeployed into higher-value, judgment-heavy work?

CHAPTER EIGHTEEN

How Businesses Will Use AI to Reduce Cost

A person unbundles their role to protect their value. A business unbundles its work for a colder reason: to spend less on it. Understanding the logic is not cynicism; it is foresight. The moves a company will make to reduce cost are largely predictable, and a person who can see them coming can position ahead of them instead of being surprised by them.

The Logic of Cost

Most organizations adopt AI for one dominant reason: to produce the same output for less, or more output for the same. Everything else, the talk of innovation and transformation, ultimately serves that arithmetic. This is not villainy; it is the basic pressure every business operates under, and competition makes it close to mandatory. A firm that can deliver the same service at half the cost will, and a firm that refuses will be undercut by one that does not. So the question for any individual is not whether their employer will pursue these savings, but how, and where the savings will come from.

It is worth holding this without bitterness. A business is not a family, however much the language of culture suggests otherwise, and expecting it to forgo large savings out of loyalty is a way of being repeatedly surprised. The clear-eyed stance is neither cynical nor naive: it accepts that an organization will act on its incentives, and uses that predictability to prepare. A person who knows the savings are coming, and roughly from where, has time to make themselves part of what the organization still needs rather than part of what it is about to trim.

Fewer People, More Output

The most direct lever is labour. If a tool lets five people do the work of eight, the saving is three salaries, and businesses will reach for it. This rarely looks like a dramatic mass layoff. More often it is quiet: a hiring freeze, a departure that is not backfilled, a vacancy simply absorbed by the tools and the people who remain. The expectation of output per person rises steadily, and the team that once felt fully staffed finds itself doing more with fewer, often without any single decisive announcement that this is what is happening.

Faster Cycles, Less Waste

Beyond headcount, AI compresses time. Work that took a week takes a day; review cycles shorten; the back-and-forth that consumed hours collapses. Faster cycles are valuable in themselves, but they also change how many people a process needs, because much of the labour in any organization is spent waiting, coordinating, and reworking. When a tool removes the waiting and catches the errors earlier, whole categories of effort, and the roles built on them, quietly become unnecessary. Efficiency at this level does not announce itself as disruption, but it is.

AI-First Operations

The deepest version is not adding AI to existing processes but redesigning the processes around AI from the start. An AI-first operation does not ask how a tool can speed up the current way of working; it asks what the work would look like if built around the tools from the ground up. These redesigns tend to be the most consequential, because they do not preserve the old structure with a tool bolted on. They rethink it, and in rethinking it, they often find that whole layers of the old way existed only to manage limitations the tools have removed.

The clearest sign of an AI-first redesign is a layer that simply vanishes. When a process is rebuilt around the tools, the roles whose entire purpose was to compensate for the old way's slowness or error, the expediters, the checkers, the people who chased information between silos, can disappear, because the problem they solved no longer exists. This is why redesign is more disruptive than adoption: adoption speeds up the existing roles, while redesign can erase the reason some of them existed in the first place.

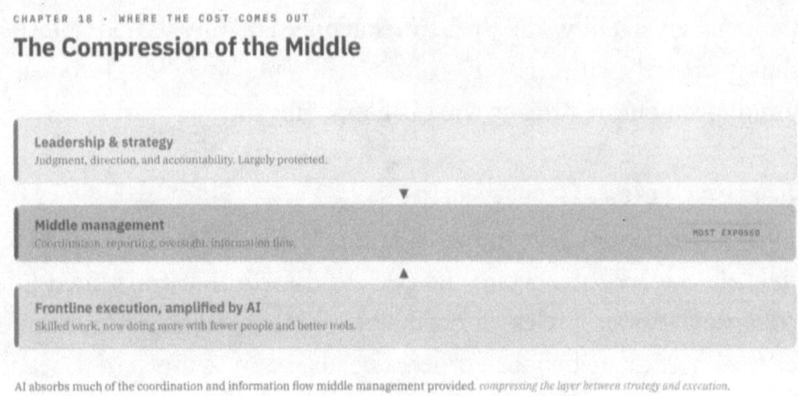

Figure 18.1 *The Compression of the Middle: AI absorbs the coordination that justified the middle layer.*

The Pressure on the Middle

One layer feels this more than any other: the middle. A great deal of middle management exists to move information up and down, to coordinate between teams, to compile reports, and to translate strategy into tasks and results back into summaries. This is precisely the kind of work, gathering, summarizing, routing, scheduling, that AI does well and cheaply. When the tools absorb the coordination, the layer that existed to provide it is compressed, caught between a leadership tier that sets direction and a frontline tier that does the work, with less of the connective tissue that used to justify its size.

This does not mean management disappears. The part of management that is genuine judgment, developing people, making hard calls, owning outcomes, holding accountability, is as valuable as ever. But the part that is pure coordination and information-passing is exposed, and the managers most at risk are the ones whose role is mostly the latter. The squeeze falls hardest on the middle that only moves information, not the middle that exercises judgment.

For a manager reading this, the path is specific. It means deliberately shifting weight from the coordinating work the tools now do toward the work they cannot: making genuine decisions under uncertainty, developing the people on the team, building the relationships that hold things together, and standing behind outcomes. A manager who lets the tools handle the reporting and reinvests that time in judgment and people is moving out of the compressed zone. One who clings to the coordination as proof of being busy is standing exactly where the floor is thinnest.

What This Means for a Person

Read defensively, this map is a warning; read well, it is a guide. If the savings come from headcount, faster cycles, redesigned operations, and a compressed middle, then the safer ground is clear enough. It lies at the top, in genuine judgment and accountability, and at the skilled frontline, in work amplified rather than replaced by tools. The riskiest place to stand is the pure-coordination middle, doing work whose whole purpose is to pass information that the tools now pass on their own.

None of this is a reason for despair, but it is a reason to position deliberately. A person who understands how businesses capture savings can move toward the protected layers before the compression reaches them, deepening the judgment that leadership rewards or the skilled execution the frontline needs. To do any of that, though, requires the ability to learn new things quickly and continuously, and that ability is itself being transformed, which is the subject of the final chapter of this part.

IN PRACTICE

A regional operations manager spent most of his week on coordination: pulling numbers from a dozen teams, compiling them into reports, relaying decisions downward and results upward, and keeping everyone aligned. When his company rolled out tools that gathered and summarized that information automatically, he felt the floor shift. The very work that justified his position was being done, instantly and for almost nothing, by software.

He understood the compression before it reached him, and read the org map honestly. The pure coordination was going; what remained valuable was judgment, the calls that required understanding the business, and the development of the people on his teams. So he deliberately moved his weight toward those: making the hard prioritization decisions, coaching his frontline leads, owning outcomes rather than relaying them. When the company did flatten its middle layer, he was no longer sitting in the part that got compressed. He had moved, in time, to the part that still mattered.

IN SHORT

- Businesses adopt AI mainly to reduce cost: the same output for less, or more output for the same.
- The savings come from fewer people for more output, faster cycles, less waste, and operations redesigned around AI from the start.
- These changes rarely arrive as dramatic layoffs; more often as freezes, unfilled vacancies, and steadily rising output expectations.
- Middle management is the most exposed layer, because much of its work is the coordination and information flow AI now handles cheaply.

- The safer ground is judgment and accountability at the top and skilled, AI-amplified execution at the frontline; the pure-coordination middle is the risk.

ASK YOURSELF

1. Which cost levers, fewer people, faster cycles, less waste, or redesigned operations, is a given employer most likely to pull?
2. How much of a role is genuine judgment and accountability, and how much is pure coordination or information-passing?
3. Does a role sit in the protected top or frontline, or in the exposed coordinating middle?
4. What would moving toward the judgment-heavy or skilled-execution layers involve, starting now?

CHAPTER NINETEEN
How Learning Itself Is Changing

Every response to disruption discussed so far, upgrading a role, unbundling tasks, moving toward complementary work, rests on a single underlying ability: the ability to learn new things, quickly and repeatedly. That ability has always mattered. What is new is that the way learning itself works is changing, and the old model, the one most people were raised on, is becoming a weaker fit for the world they now have to navigate.

Why the Old Model Is Weakening

The traditional model treated learning as a phase: study first, in school or a course or a certification, then apply what was learned across a long, stable career. It worked when knowledge was scarce, expensive to access, and slow to change. A degree could anchor decades of work because the field it covered moved slowly. None of those conditions holds as firmly now. Knowledge is abundant and nearly free to access, skills change within years rather than decades, and a credential earned once is a weaker guarantee of present capability. The model is not useless, but it is no longer sufficient on its own.

From Knowledge to Application

The first shift is from knowing to applying. When information was scarce, knowing things was itself valuable, and education concentrated on transferring knowledge into heads. But when a tool can supply almost any fact or explanation on demand, the scarce and valuable skill is no longer knowing; it is judging, deciding, and applying knowledge well in a specific situation. Learning, accordingly, has to shift its emphasis from acquiring information toward building the judgment to use it, which is a different and harder kind of learning that cannot simply be downloaded.

From Certificates to Outcomes

The second shift is from credentials to demonstrated capability. A certificate was always a proxy, a signal that a person had probably acquired certain skills. As the link between credentials and present capability loosens, the proxy matters less and the thing itself matters more. What a person can actually do, shown through real work, a portfolio, a track record of outcomes, increasingly speaks louder than what they once studied. This is not the end of credentials, but it is the rise of evidence: the demonstration of capability is becoming its own qualification.

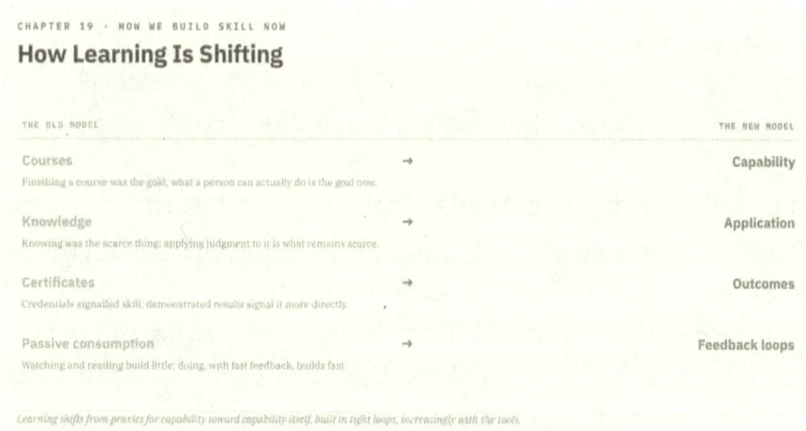

Figure 19.1 *How Learning Is Shifting: from proxies for capability toward capability itself.*

From Passive Consumption to Feedback Loops

The third shift is in how learning actually happens. Passive consumption, watching a lecture, reading a book, following along, feels like learning but builds capability slowly, because understanding something is not the same as being able to do it. Capability is built in feedback loops: attempting something, seeing what worked and what did not, and adjusting. The tighter and faster the loop, the faster the learning. This is why a week of doing often teaches more than a month of watching, and why the most effective learning has always been active rather than passive.

Here, unexpectedly, the tools help. An AI can act as a tireless practice partner and critic: posing problems, reviewing attempts, explaining mistakes, and giving immediate feedback on demand. The same technology disrupting the work can dramatically accelerate the learning, by collapsing the feedback loop from days to seconds and giving almost anyone access to the kind of responsive coaching that was once scarce and expensive.

The practical version of this is humble and powerful. A person learning a new skill can now attempt real work immediately, ask a tool to critique the result, and act on the critique within minutes, then repeat. What once required a mentor's scarce time or an expensive course is available continuously, to anyone, at the moment of need. The bottleneck on learning has historically been access to feedback, and for the motivated, that bottleneck has largely dissolved.

Learning With the Tools, Not Around Them

This points to a new literacy: learning to learn with AI rather than in spite of it. There is a real temptation to use the tools as a shortcut that skips the learning entirely, letting the machine produce the answer so the person never has to build the capability. That is a trap, because it leaves the person dependent and un-improved. Used well, the same tool does the opposite: it becomes an accelerator of one's own capability, a way to practise more, get feedback faster, and reach competence sooner. The difference is whether the tool is used to avoid thinking or to get better at it.

The Continuous Stance

Underneath all three shifts is a single change in posture. Learning is no longer a phase that ends when work begins; it is a continuous activity woven through a working life, because the half-life of any specific skill keeps shrinking. The person who learns once and coasts is on borrowed time; the person who treats learning as a permanent, ongoing part of the job is the one who keeps adapting as the ground moves. This is less a technique than a stance, a way of holding a career as something always under construction rather than ever finished.

That stance, learning continuously, applying rather than merely knowing, building capability in tight loops with the tools, is the foundation everything else rests on. It is also the bridge to the heart of this book. The parts so far have explained why AI disrupts, what it changes, when it lands, where it hits, and how it actually works. What remains is the method: a repeatable loop for turning all of this understanding into deliberate action. That method is the subject of Part Six.

IN PRACTICE

A junior data analyst had always learned the way she was taught to: enrolling in courses, collecting certificates, and working through material before trying to apply any of it. The trouble was that by the time she finished a course, the tools it covered had often moved on, and she could recite concepts she could not yet use. The old model was failing her in real time.

She changed her approach to match the new reality. Instead of studying first and applying later, she picked real problems and learned by building, using an AI tool as a tireless tutor that posed challenges, reviewed her work, and explained her mistakes the moment she made them. The feedback loop that had once taken a teacher a week now took seconds. Within months she could do more than peers who held more certificates, because she had been building capability directly rather than collecting proxies for it. She had stopped preparing to learn and started simply learning, continuously, in the middle of the work.

IN SHORT

- Every response to disruption rests on the ability to learn quickly and continuously, and the way learning works is itself changing.
- The old model, study once then apply for decades, fits a world of scarce, stable knowledge that no longer exists.
- Learning is shifting from knowledge to application, from certificates to demonstrated outcomes, and from passive consumption to tight feedback loops.
- The same tools that disrupt the work can accelerate the learning, by collapsing feedback loops and acting as an on-demand practice partner.
- The deepest shift is a stance: learning as a continuous part of working life rather than a phase that ends when a career begins.

ASK YOURSELF

1. Does current learning emphasize acquiring knowledge, or building the judgment to apply it?
2. What demonstrated outcome or piece of real work would show present capability better than a credential?
3. Where could a tight feedback loop, doing and adjusting, replace passive consumption?
4. Are the tools being used as a shortcut that skips learning, or as an accelerator that deepens it?

PART SIX

HOW

How to Escape: The Agile Reinvention Loop

Reinvention is not a single leap but a loop: expose the work, shed the waste, climb to higher value, augment with AI, prove the result, and evolve, then run it again.

CHAPTER TWENTY

Run Your Career Like an Agile Team

The previous parts diagnosed the problem: why AI is different, what it changes, when it lands, where it hits, and how it actually works. This part turns diagnosis into method. The central idea is simple and, once seen, hard to unsee: reinvention is not a single dramatic leap but a loop, run continuously, the way a good agile team builds a product. The rest of this part is that loop, broken into six repeatable steps.

From One Big Leap to a Continuous Loop

Most people imagine career reinvention as a wrenching, one-time event: quit, retrain, emerge transformed. That model is slow, risky, and badly suited to a world that keeps moving. If the ground shifts every couple of years, a single leap lands a person on terrain that has already changed again. The alternative is to stop treating reinvention as an event and start treating it as a practice, a loop that runs in the background of a working life, making small, continuous adjustments rather than rare, violent ones.

What Agile Teaches a Career

Software teams faced a version of this problem decades ago. Long, detailed plans failed because requirements changed faster than the plans could be executed, so they invented agile: work in short cycles, let evidence rather than the plan drive decisions, pull work as capacity allows rather than pushing it on a fixed schedule, and let the team organize itself around the goal. Each of these translates directly to a career under disruption.

Short cycles mean reinventing in small increments, not waiting for a grand plan. Empirical process means letting real evidence, what actually works and what AI can really do, override assumption and ego. Pull over push means taking on change at a sustainable rate rather than on a panic schedule. And self-organization means owning the direction rather than waiting for an employer to assign it. A career run this way is not a fixed plan being executed but a loop being iterated.

The ESCAPE Loop

The loop at the heart of this book has six steps, and they spell ESCAPE. Expose the reality of the work. Shed what no longer creates value. Climb toward higher-value capability. Augment that capability with AI. Prove the value so others can see it. And evolve, building resilience and starting the loop again. Each of the chapters that follows is one of these steps, and the order matters less than the fact that it never stops.

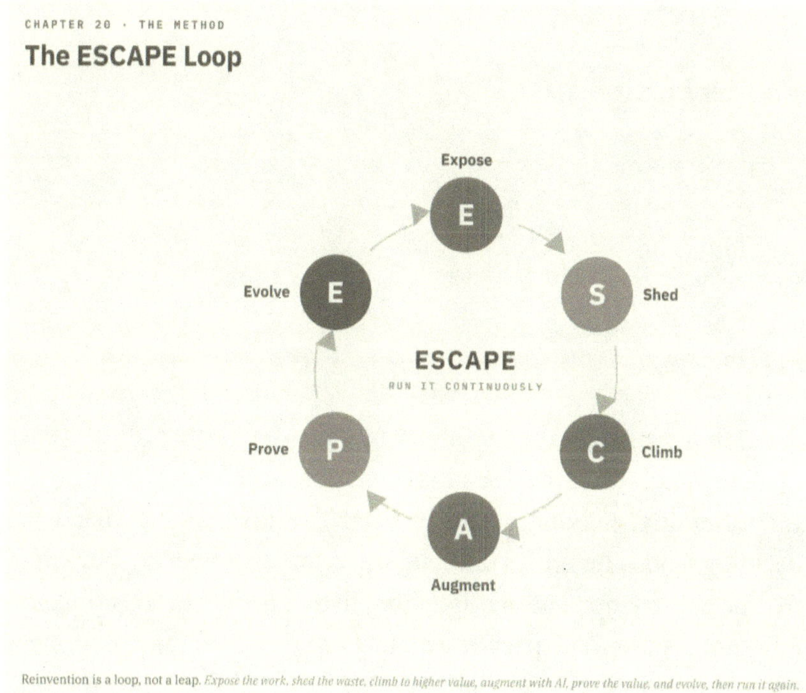

Figure 20.1 *The ESCAPE Loop: six repeating steps for continuous reinvention.*

What makes it a loop rather than a checklist is the final step. Evolving is not a finish line; it feeds straight back into exposing the work again, because by the time a person has climbed and proven value, the ground has moved and the audit is due once more. Run once, the steps are a useful exercise. Run continuously, they become a way of holding a career that disruption cannot easily catch off guard.

The OODA Loop and the Speed of Adaptation

There is an older, sharper version of this idea from a fighter pilot and strategist named John Boyd, who observed that in any fast-changing contest, the side that cycles through a simple loop faster tends to win. His loop was Observe, Orient, Decide, Act, and the insight was that speed of iteration, not size of plan, decides outcomes. The lesson for an AI-era career is direct: whoever can observe, make sense, decide, and act faster adapts first.

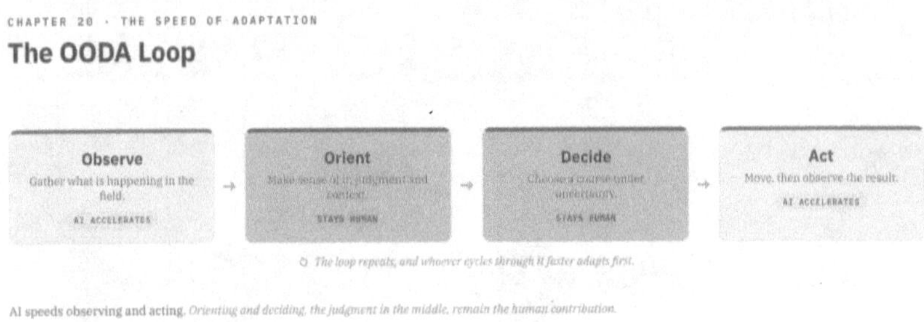

Figure 20.2 *The OODA Loop: AI speeds observing and acting; orienting and deciding stay human.*

Here AI changes the math in a specific way. It dramatically speeds up observing, the gathering of information, and acting, the execution. But orienting, making sense of what the information means, and deciding, choosing under uncertainty, remain stubbornly human. The middle of the loop is where judgment lives, and it is exactly the part AI does not replace. The person who lets AI accelerate the observing and the acting, while owning the orienting and deciding, runs the fastest loop of all.

Why a Loop Beats a Plan

Under deep uncertainty, a detailed plan is a liability, because it commits to assumptions that the next development will break. A loop makes no such commitment. It assumes the world will change and builds the changing-in-response directly into how a person works. A plan asks what will happen and bets on the answer; a loop asks what is happening now and adjusts. In a stable world the plan wins on efficiency. In this one, the loop wins on adaptability, and adaptability is the whole game.

The six chapters that follow walk the loop one step at a time, from the first honest audit to the resilience that comes from running it for years. None of the steps is complicated on its own. The discipline is in running them together, and in running them again. The loop begins where all honest change begins, with seeing the work clearly, which is the first step: Expose.

IN PRACTICE

A freelance brand strategist had always reinvented herself in painful lurches: every few years, a sudden realization that her skills were dated, followed by a frantic scramble to catch up. By the time she caught up, the field had moved again, and the cycle of panic simply repeated.

She decided to run her practice like an agile team instead. Each month became a short cycle with one small reinvention goal: a tool to learn, a service to test, a skill to deepen. She let evidence from real client work decide what to keep, and she stopped waiting for a crisis to force change. The lurches disappeared. Reinvention stopped being a periodic emergency and became a quiet, continuous background process, and for the first time her skills stayed current without the panic that had always accompanied keeping them so.

IN SHORT

- Reinvention works best not as a single dramatic leap but as a continuous loop, run like an agile team.

- Agile lessons translate to a career: short cycles, evidence over plans, a sustainable pace, and owning one's own direction.
- The ESCAPE Loop has six repeating steps: Expose, Shed, Climb, Augment, Prove, and Evolve.
- Boyd's OODA Loop shows that speed of iteration wins; AI accelerates observing and acting, while orienting and deciding stay human.
- Under deep uncertainty a loop beats a plan, because it builds continuous adaptation into how a person works.

ASK YOURSELF

1. Is reinvention currently being treated as a rare, dramatic leap or as a continuous, low-key loop?
2. Which agile habit, short cycles, evidence over plans, sustainable pace, or self-direction, is most missing from how a career is being run?
3. Where could AI accelerate the observing and acting, leaving more room for the human orienting and deciding?
4. What would running one short reinvention cycle this month actually involve?

CHAPTER TWENTY-ONE

Step One: Audit Your Current Work

Every loop begins with seeing clearly, and most people never look at their own work closely enough to change it well. The first step, Expose, is an honest, empirical audit of the actual work: not the job description, but the real tasks that fill a real week, examined for what they are rather than what a person wishes they were.

Start With the Truth

Reinvention fails most often not at the doing but at the seeing. People defend the work they are proud of, overlook the work that quietly fills their days, and assume rather than test what AI can do. The audit is a deliberate cure for all three. It replaces a vague sense of a job with a concrete inventory, and it insists that the inventory be honest, even where honesty is uncomfortable.

Four Questions for Every Task

The audit runs four questions across every task in the inventory. Is it repetitive, following a pattern? Does it require real judgment? Does it create value that others would actually pay for or miss if it stopped? And can AI already do it, tested rather than guessed? The four answers sort each task far more reliably than any gut feeling, because they separate the dimensions people usually blur together: how routine a task is, how valuable it is, and how exposed it is.

The Audit Grid

Two of those questions, the value a task creates and how well AI can already do it, can be crossed into a simple grid that makes the next move obvious.

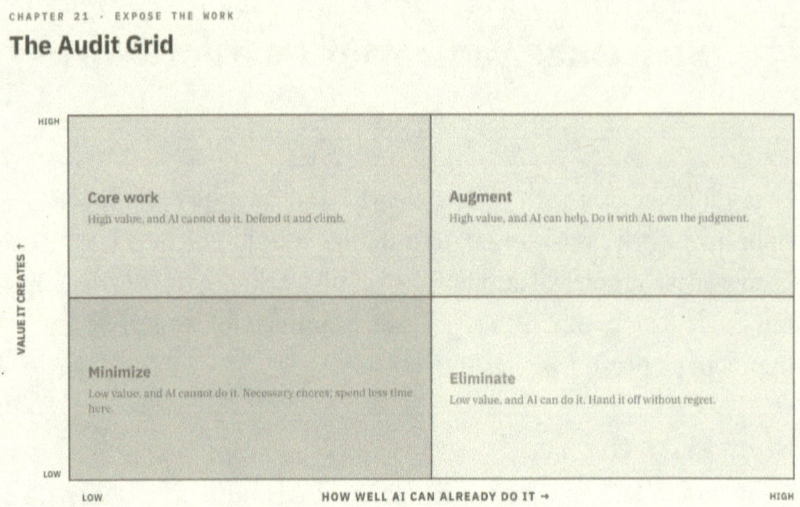

Figure 21.1 *The Audit Grid: cross the value a task creates against what AI can already do.*

The high-value work AI cannot do is the core: defend it and climb. The high-value work AI can help with is where to augment, doing it with the tool while owning the judgment. The low-value work AI can do should be eliminated, handed off without a second thought. And the low-value work AI cannot yet do is to be minimized, done quickly and grudgingly, never mistaken for the real job. One grid, four clear instructions.

Evidence, Not Ego

The audit only works if evidence, not ego, decides. The ego protects the work a person is proud of, especially the hard-won craft that may no longer create much value, and it dismisses the tools without testing them. The discipline is to actually try the tool on the task before judging it, and to ask honestly whether a piece of work still creates value or merely still feels important. The tasks people most resist auditing are usually the ones the audit most needs to reach.

Shed the Waste

Seeing clearly is only useful if it is followed by shedding. Once the audit reveals the low-value and the automatable, the next move is to stop doing it, deliberately, to free the capacity the rest of the loop requires. Most people carry a surprising amount of work that creates little value and persists only out of habit. Cutting it is not laziness; it is what makes room to climb. A person who audits but never sheds simply piles new work on old and burns out before the loop can help.

The audit, run honestly and followed by shedding, clears the ground. It shows what to defend, what to drop, and where the capacity for the next step will come from. That next step is to build the capability that turns freed time into rising value: the advantage stack.

IN PRACTICE

A financial analyst sat down and listed every task in a typical week, honestly, and was unsettled by what she saw. Most of her hours went to gathering data, building standard reports, and reconciling figures, all of which a tool could now largely do. The work she was proudest of, the analysis that actually informed decisions, occupied a surprisingly small share of her time.

Rather than defend the comfortable routine, she let the grid decide. The report-building and data-gathering were high-effort but low in the value only she could add, and increasingly automatable, so she handed them to the tools. She minimized the necessary chores and poured the reclaimed hours into the interpretation and judgment that sat in her core. Within a quarter she was doing less work and more valuable work, and the audit, uncomfortable as it had been, was what made the shift possible.

IN SHORT

- The loop begins with Expose: an honest, empirical audit of the real tasks that fill a week.

- Four questions sort each task: is it repetitive, does it need judgment, does it create value, and can AI already do it?
- The Audit Grid crosses value against AI capability, giving four clear moves: defend the core, augment, minimize, or eliminate.
- Evidence, not ego, should decide; test the tool on a task before judging it, and question work that feels important but creates little value.
- Seeing must be followed by shedding: deliberately dropping the low-value and automatable work to free capacity for the climb.

ASK YOURSELF

1 Listed honestly, how is a typical week actually spent, task by task?

2 Plotted on the Audit Grid, which tasks are core, which to augment, which to minimize, and which to eliminate?

3 Which task is being defended out of pride rather than because it still creates real value?

4 What low-value or automatable work could be shed this cycle to free capacity for the climb?

CHAPTER TWENTY-TWO

Step Two: Build Your AI Advantage Stack

Shedding the low-value work frees capacity, and the question becomes what to do with it. The answer is to climb: to build the stack of capabilities that compound into an advantage AI cannot easily erode. No single skill does this anymore. What protects and elevates a career is a stack of complementary capabilities, each amplifying the others.

Advantage Is a Stack, Not a Skill

The search for the one skill that guarantees safety, the right programming language, the right certification, is a search for something that no longer exists. Any single skill can be learned by others or absorbed by tools. Durable advantage comes instead from a stack: several capabilities that, combined, are far harder to copy or automate than any one of them alone. The goal is not to be the best at one thing but to be the rare combination of several.

The Six Layers

The stack for an AI era has six layers, each building on the one below.

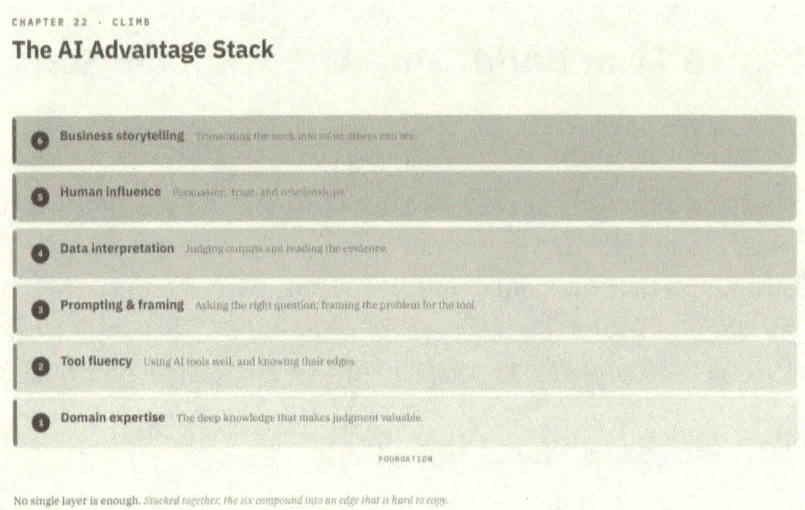

Figure 22.1 *The AI Advantage Stack: six layers that compound into an edge no single skill provides.*

At the base sits domain expertise, the deep knowledge of a field that makes a person's judgment worth trusting. On it rests tool fluency, the practical ability to use AI tools well and know their limits. Above that come prompting and problem framing, the skill of asking the right question and shaping a problem so a tool can help with it, and data interpretation, the judgment to evaluate what the tool returns. The top two layers are the most human: influence, the persuasion and trust that move people, and business storytelling, the ability to translate work into value others can see. Each layer multiplies the value of the rest.

Why the Stack Compounds

The power of the stack is that its layers multiply rather than add. Domain expertise without tool fluency is slow; tool fluency without domain expertise is shallow; both without influence and storytelling stay invisible. A person who has all six is not six times more valuable but something closer to exponentially so, because the combination is genuinely scarce. Tools can supply any single layer cheaply. The integrated stack, sitting in one person's judgment, is what stays hard to replace.

Building It Deliberately

A stack is built one layer at a time, and the loop makes that practical. Rather than trying to improve everything at once, a person can identify the weakest or most limiting layer and strengthen it in a single cycle, then reassess. An expert with deep domain knowledge but no tool fluency climbs fastest by learning the tools; a fluent tool user with shallow domain knowledge climbs fastest by going deeper into a field. The stack is personal, and the next layer to build is usually the one whose absence is currently holding the rest back.

Climbing builds the capability. But capability applied task by task leaves most of its value on the table, because the largest gains come from redesigning the whole system of work, not from speeding up its parts. That is the next step: thinking in systems, and augmenting them with AI.

> **IN PRACTICE**
>
> An SEO specialist watched the tools absorb the keyword research and content drafting that had been the core of his job, and briefly assumed his single specialty was finished. Looked at as one skill, it was. Looked at as a stack, it was not.
>
> He set about building the layers. On top of his domain knowledge of how search worked, he added real fluency with the new tools, then the framing skill to direct them well, then the judgment to interpret what they produced, and finally the ability to translate all of it into business results his clients could see. Any one layer was now cheap. The combination, sitting in one person who understood search, tools, framing, interpretation, and storytelling together, was rare and valuable, and it made him more sought-after than he had been when his single specialty was scarce.

IN SHORT

- Durable advantage comes from a stack of capabilities, not a single skill that others can learn or tools can absorb.
- The AI advantage stack has six layers: domain expertise, tool fluency, prompting and framing, data interpretation, human influence, and business storytelling.
- The layers multiply rather than add; the integrated combination in one person is genuinely scarce.
- Tools can supply any single layer cheaply, but not the whole stack sitting in one person's judgment.
- Build the stack deliberately, one layer per cycle, starting with whichever weak layer is holding the rest back.

ASK YOURSELF

1. Of the six layers, which are already strong, and which are weak or missing?
2. Which single layer, if strengthened, would most increase the value of the others?
3. Where is a single-skill identity creating a false sense of security, or of vulnerability?
4. What is one deliberate step this cycle toward building the weakest layer of the stack?

CHAPTER TWENTY-THREE

Step Three: Think in Systems, Not Tasks

A stronger stack of capabilities can be wasted by applying it the wrong way, one task at a time. The largest gains come from stepping back and redesigning the whole system of work, deciding which parts a human does, which a tool does, and how they fit together. This is the Augment step: not bolting AI onto old tasks, but designing a human-AI system as a single, well-run team.

The Task Trap

The natural instinct, on getting a new tool, is to speed up the tasks already being done. This is the task trap. Optimizing individual tasks yields small, local gains and often misses the point, because the biggest inefficiencies usually live between tasks, in the handoffs, the waiting, the rework, and the steps that exist only to compensate for other steps. Real improvement comes from optimizing the whole system, not its pieces.

Map the System

Systems thinking starts with a map. What are the inputs, what are the steps, where does value actually get created, and where does it get stuck? Almost every workflow has a bottleneck, a single step that limits the whole, and speeding up anything other than the bottleneck changes nothing. Mapping the system reveals the leverage points: the few places where a change actually moves the outcome, as opposed to the many places where effort feels productive but the system as a whole does not improve.

Designing the Human-AI Workflow

With the system mapped, the design question becomes which steps belong to the human, which to the tool, and how the handoffs work. The aim is to treat human and AI as one cross-functional team, each doing what it does best: the tool handling scale, speed, and first drafts; the human handling judgment, exceptions, and accountability. A well-designed workflow is not a person occasionally using a tool but a deliberate division of labour with clean handoffs between the two.

Three Levels of Oversight

A key design choice is how much human oversight each step needs, and there are three levels to choose from.

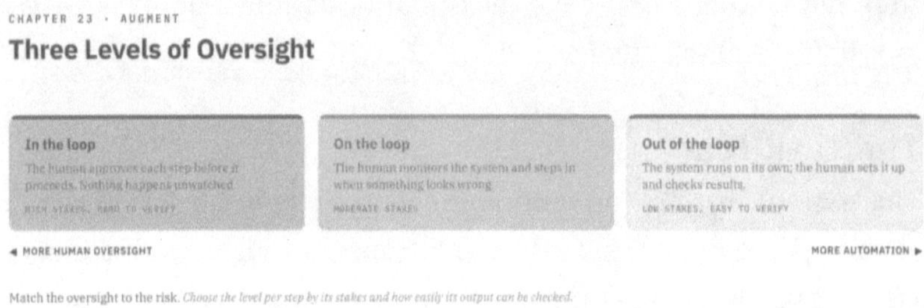

Figure 23.1 *Three levels of oversight: match how closely a human watches to the stakes of the step.*

When stakes are high or the output is hard to verify, the human stays in the loop, approving each step before it proceeds. When stakes are moderate, the human moves on the loop, monitoring the system and intervening when something looks wrong. And when stakes are low and the output is easy to check, the human can step out of the loop entirely, setting the system up and reviewing results. The mistake is to apply one level everywhere: to babysit trivial tasks, or to leave high-stakes ones unwatched. The skill is matching the oversight to the risk, step by step.

Optimize the Whole

Throughout, the measure of success is the output of the whole system, not the speed of any single step. A workflow where every individual task is fast but the handoffs leak time is worse than one with a slower step and a smoother flow. Designing for the whole, rather than optimizing the parts, is what turns a stack of capabilities into a genuine multiplier.

A redesigned, augmented system can produce far more value than before. But value that no one sees does not protect a career, and in a world where output is cheap, demonstrated value matters more than ever. The next step is making that value visible: Prove.

IN PRACTICE

A customer success manager started, as most people do, by using AI to speed up individual tasks: drafting replies faster, summarizing calls more quickly. The gains were real but small, and the underlying work felt as overloaded as ever.

When she stepped back and mapped her whole system, the picture changed. The bottleneck was not the speed of any single task but the handoffs between onboarding, support, and renewal, where information was lost and customers fell through the gaps. She redesigned the workflow as a human-AI team: the tools watching for at-risk accounts and drafting routine outreach on the loop, while she stayed firmly in the loop for the high-stakes renewal conversations and the judgment calls. Optimizing the whole system, rather than its parts, did far more than any individual speed-up had, and her accounts noticed the difference.

IN SHORT

- The biggest gains come from redesigning the whole system of work, not from speeding up individual tasks.
- Map the system to find its bottleneck and leverage points; improving anything but the bottleneck changes little.
- Design the human-AI workflow as one team: the tool for scale and drafts, the human for judgment, exceptions, and accountability.

- Match oversight to risk: human in the loop for high stakes, on the loop for moderate, out of the loop for low-stakes, easily verified work.
- Optimize for the output of the whole system, not the speed of any single step.

ASK YOURSELF

1. Is effort going into speeding up individual tasks rather than redesigning the whole system?
2. Mapped end to end, where is the real bottleneck in the work, and is effort aimed at it?
3. Which steps should have a human in the loop, which on the loop, and which can run out of it?
4. What handoff or bottleneck, if redesigned, would most improve the output of the whole system?

CHAPTER TWENTY-FOUR

Step Four: Make Your Value Visible

It is possible to run the loop well, build a strong stack, design an excellent system, and still be overlooked, because the value created is invisible to the people who decide. The Prove step closes that gap. In an era when output is cheap and abundant, the scarce and decisive thing is demonstrated value, shown through outcomes rather than claimed through words.

Invisible Value Is Vulnerable Value

Value that no one can see does not protect a person, however real it is. When organizations look to cut cost, the work they cannot see the value of goes first, regardless of how much that work quietly mattered. This is uncomfortable for people who believe good work should speak for itself. It rarely does. Making value visible is not self-promotion for its own sake; it is the difference between value that protects a career and value that quietly fails to.

Outcomes Over Claims

The unit of proof is the outcome, not the claim. Saying one is valuable persuades no one; showing what changed because of the work persuades everyone. There is a ladder here, from activity to impact, and most people stop too low on it.

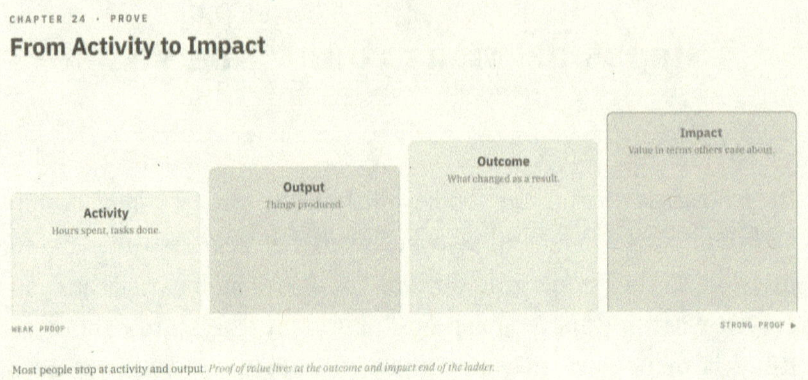

Figure 24.1 *From activity to impact: proof of value lives at the higher rungs of the ladder.*

Activity, the hours spent, proves the least. Output, the things produced, proves a little more. Outcomes, what actually changed as a result, prove a great deal. And impact, that change expressed in terms the business genuinely cares about, proves the most. The same work can be described at any rung, and the higher the rung, the more visible and durable its value. The discipline is to always climb the ladder, to push past activity and output toward the outcome and impact that others recognize as worth paying for.

Small, Visible Wins

Proof is best delivered the way agile teams deliver software: incrementally, in small, visible wins, rather than saved up for one grand reveal. A steady stream of modest, demonstrated results builds a reputation more reliably than a single large project that lands all at once or not at all. Frequent small proof also compounds trust, so that when a bigger claim must be made, it rests on a track record rather than a promise.

Build a Proof Trail

Over time, these visible wins become a proof trail: a record of before-and-after impact, short case studies, and concrete examples of value delivered. This trail is an asset in itself. It makes a person's contribution legible to others, it travels with them between roles, and it turns the abstract claim of being valuable into a documented pattern of having been. Keeping the trail is a small, ongoing habit that pays off precisely when it matters most.

Proving value makes the loop visible to others. The final two steps make it visible and sustainable to the person running it: tracking the reinvention itself, and building the optionality that turns one good loop into lasting resilience. That begins with making the invisible progress visible.

> **IN PRACTICE**
> A data scientist did excellent work that almost no one understood. He built models that quietly saved the company a great deal, but he described his work in the language of activity and output, the techniques used and the models built, and to the people who set budgets, it was invisible.
>
> He learned to climb the ladder from activity to impact. Instead of reporting which algorithm he had used, he reported what had changed because of it, and then what that change was worth in the terms his executives cared about. He delivered the proof in small, frequent wins rather than one annual summary, and he kept a simple trail of before-and-after results. The work itself did not change; its visibility did. When the next round of cost-cutting came, his value was one of the few things in the building that everyone could see, and it protected him.

IN SHORT

- Value that no one can see does not protect a career; in an era of cheap output, demonstrated value is decisive.
- Proof comes from outcomes, not claims; climb the ladder from activity to output to outcome to business impact.

- Deliver proof in small, frequent, visible wins rather than saving it for one grand reveal.
- Keep a proof trail of before-and-after results and short case studies; it travels with a person between roles.
- Making value visible is not vanity; it is what separates value that protects a career from value that quietly fails to.

ASK YOURSELF

1. Is the value of current work visible to the people who decide, or only known to the person doing it?
2. On the ladder from activity to impact, how high are contributions usually described, and could they climb higher?
3. Where could a small, visible win be delivered soon rather than saved for one large reveal?
4. What before-and-after results could begin a proof trail that travels between roles?

CHAPTER TWENTY-FIVE

Step Five: Visualize Your Progress

Reinvention is hard to sustain because it is invisible. Unlike a project with a deadline, the slow work of auditing, climbing, and augmenting produces no obvious marker of progress, and what cannot be seen is easily abandoned. The fifth step borrows another agile practice: make the work visible to the person doing it, so the loop keeps turning at a steady, sustainable pace.

Making the Invisible Visible

A reinvention happening only in someone's head tends to stall. There is no sense of momentum, no record of what has been tried, no obvious next thing to pick up. Making the work visible, on a simple board, converts a vague intention into concrete, moving pieces. It is the same reason teams put their work on a wall: visibility creates momentum, accountability, and the small satisfaction of watching things move toward done.

The Personal Reinvention Board

The tool is a personal Kanban board, no more complex than three columns: a backlog of what to try, what is in progress this cycle, and what is done.

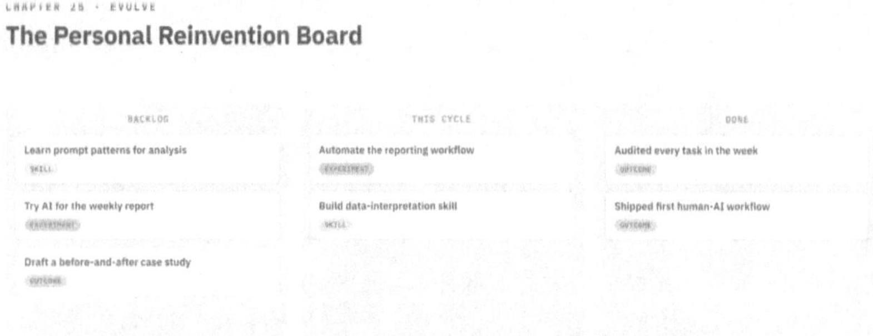

Make the invisible visible. *A simple board for skills, experiments, and outcomes keeps reinvention moving at a sustainable pace*

Figure 25.1 *The Personal Reinvention Board: a simple Kanban for skills, experiments, and outcomes.*

The cards are the substance of the loop: skills to build, experiments to run, and outcomes to capture. Moving a card from backlog to this cycle to done makes the reinvention tangible, and the board doubles as a record of how far a person has actually come, which is easy to lose sight of in the day-to-day. The point is not the tool, which can be a wall of sticky notes or a simple app, but the visibility it creates.

Respect the Timebox

A loop is only sustainable at a sustainable pace. The temptation, especially when disruption feels urgent, is to attempt everything at once and burn out within weeks. Agile teams guard against this with the timebox: a fixed, modest amount of work per cycle, protected from overload. A career loop needs the same discipline. Consistency over months beats intensity over days, and the board helps enforce it by making overload visible before it becomes exhaustion.

Run Retros on Yourself

The final habit is the retrospective: at the end of each cycle, a short, honest review of what worked, what did not, and what to change next time. Agile teams improve not by working harder but by inspecting and adapting their own process regularly, and a person can do the same to their own reinvention. Running a retro on oneself turns the loop from a fixed routine into something that gets better each time it runs, which is what evolving actually means.

Visualizing and pacing the loop keeps it turning for the long haul. Run for long enough, the loop produces something larger than any single skill or role: a portfolio of capabilities, proof, and options that together make a career genuinely resilient. Building that resilience deliberately is the final step.

IN PRACTICE

A junior product manager kept meaning to reinvent himself for an AI-shaped industry, and kept not doing it. The intention lived only in his head, where it produced guilt but no progress, and every busy week pushed it further off.

He built himself a simple board: three columns, a handful of cards for skills to learn and experiments to run. Suddenly the abstract intention had concrete pieces he could move. He limited himself to two cards per cycle, protecting a sustainable pace, and ended each cycle with a short, honest review of what had worked. The board did what willpower had not: it made his progress visible, kept it moving, and, by forcing him to reflect each cycle, made the process itself a little better each time. Months later, he was startled to look back at the done column and see how far the small, steady moves had carried him.

IN SHORT

- Reinvention stalls because it is invisible; making it visible to oneself keeps the loop turning.
- A personal Kanban board with backlog, this-cycle, and done columns turns a vague intention into moving pieces.
- The cards are the substance of the loop: skills to build, experiments to run, and outcomes to capture.
- Respect the timebox: a modest, protected amount of work per cycle, because consistency beats intensity and prevents burnout.
- Run retrospectives on oneself each cycle, inspecting and adapting the process so the loop improves each time it runs.

ASK YOURSELF

1. Is reinvention currently living only in intention, with no visible record of progress?
2. What would the first few cards on a personal reinvention board be?
3. Is the current pace sustainable, or is it veering toward an overload the loop cannot survive?
4. What would an honest retrospective on the last few months of reinvention reveal?

CHAPTER TWENTY-SIX
Step Six: Build Career Optionality

Run the loop once and a person upgrades a role. Run it for years and something larger accumulates: a set of capabilities, relationships, and assets that together make a career resilient in a way no single job can. The last step is to build that resilience on purpose, through optionality, so that the security of a career rests on many foundations rather than one.

One Path Is Fragile

A career resting entirely on a single employer and a single income is a single point of failure, however stable it looks. When that one path is disrupted, everything goes at once. Optionality is the antidote: several live paths, so that the loss of any one is an inconvenience rather than a catastrophe. This is not disloyalty or hedging out of fear; it is the simple recognition that resilience comes from diversity, and a one-path career has none.

From Selling Time to Building Assets

The deepest shift in building optionality is from selling time to building assets.

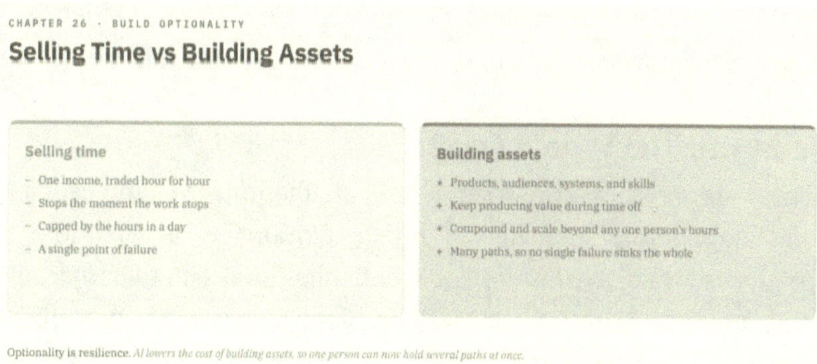

Figure 26.1 *Selling time is capped and fragile; building assets compounds into resilience.*

Selling time, the standard employment bargain, is inherently capped and fragile: it stops the moment a person stops, and it is limited by the hours in a day. Assets behave differently. A product, an audience, a body of writing, a reusable system, a reputation: these keep working when a person does not, compound over time, and scale beyond any single set of hours. A career built only on selling time is exposed; one that also builds assets has something underneath it that disruption cannot simply switch off.

The Portfolio Career

Optionality often takes the shape of a portfolio: a primary role alongside freelance work, a side project, a small product, or income from an asset. Each path is modest on its own, but together they provide both resilience and a hedge against any one being disrupted. The portfolio also feeds the loop, because each path generates its own audits, its own climbs, and its own proof, accelerating the learning across all of them.

AI-Enabled Side Businesses

AI changes the economics of building these paths. The cost and effort of creating a small product, a service, or a body of content have fallen sharply, which means a single person can now build assets that once required a team. The same tools disrupting employment also lower the barrier to building independent options, and the person who uses them that way turns a threat into the means of their own resilience. The leverage that worries an employee is available to the builder.

Running the Whole Loop

These six steps, expose, shed, climb, augment, prove, and evolve, are one loop, not a sequence to finish. Optionality is what the loop produces when it runs for long enough: the accumulated result of repeatedly auditing, shedding, climbing, augmenting, proving, and building. A person who runs the loop continuously does not arrive at a final, safe destination, because none exists. They arrive instead at a way of working that keeps producing safety, again and again, as the ground keeps moving.

The ESCAPE Loop is the method at the heart of this book, and the chapters of this part have walked its six steps. What it does not answer is how much to invest in it, and where the returns are highest: the economics of reinvention. That question, of cost, time, and return, is the subject of Part Seven.

IN PRACTICE

An instructional designer had spent fifteen years trading her hours for a salary, secure until the day her employer reorganized and her security evaporated overnight. The single path she had treated as safe turned out to be a single point of failure.

Rebuilding, she resolved never to depend on one path again. Alongside a new role, she used AI tools to build assets: a small library of templates she sold, a modest audience around her writing on learning design, and a side service she could run on her own time. None of the paths was large, but together they meant her income no longer rested on a single decision by a single employer. She had moved, deliberately, from only selling her time to also building things that kept working when she was not, and the resilience that gave her was worth more than the salary she had once thought of as safe.

IN SHORT

- Running the loop for years accumulates something larger than any role: a resilient career built on many foundations.
- A single employer and income is a single point of failure; optionality, several live paths, is the antidote.

- The deepest shift is from selling time, which is capped and fragile, to building assets, which compound and keep working.
- A portfolio career, a role plus freelance work, side projects, and small products, provides resilience and feeds the loop.
- AI lowers the cost of building independent assets, turning the same tools that threaten employment into the means of resilience.

ASK YOURSELF

1 How many genuinely independent income or capability paths does a career currently rest on?

2 Where is the line currently drawn between selling time and building assets, and could it shift?

3 What small asset, a product, an audience, a reusable system, could be started with the tools now available?

4 What would a portfolio of two or three modest paths look like, and which one could begin first?

PART SEVEN

HOW MUCH

How Much AI Disruption Costs, and How Much to Invest

Doing nothing has a price too: reinvention is an investment of time and a little money, measured by its return, and far cheaper than the cost of standing still.

CHAPTER TWENTY-SEVEN

The Cost of Doing Nothing

Reinvention has a price: hours, attention, sometimes money. Faced with that price, many people quietly decide to wait, to do nothing for now, on the assumption that doing nothing is free. It is not. The cost of inaction is real, it is usually larger than the cost of action, and it has the inconvenient habit of staying invisible until it is too large to pay comfortably. Before deciding how much to invest, it is worth being honest about the price of investing nothing.

This chapter makes the invisible cost visible, because a decision to invest only makes sense once both sides of the ledger are honest. People weigh the obvious cost of acting against an imagined zero, and unsurprisingly choose the zero. The real comparison is between two non-zero costs, one paid now and on purpose, the other paid later and by default. Naming the second cost is not a scare tactic; it is simply completing the arithmetic that inaction quietly leaves half-done.

The Invisible Price Tag

The cost of reinvention is easy to see: it shows up immediately, as time given up and effort spent. The cost of doing nothing is easy to miss, because it arrives slowly and never sends an invoice. Nothing bad happens on the first day of standing still, or the second, or for many months. This is precisely what makes inaction so tempting and so dangerous: the bill is deferred, and a deferred bill feels, in the moment, like no bill at all. The honest accounting compares not action against a free alternative, but action against the slow, compounding cost of its absence.

There is a useful parallel in physical health. The cost of exercise is immediate and obvious, while the cost of avoiding it is silent for years before arriving all at once. No one receives a monthly invoice for a sedentary life, yet the bill is real and compounding, and by the time it presents itself the price has grown enormous. Career relevance behaves the same way: cheap to maintain continuously, expensive to recover once lost.

Relevance Decays

Skills have a half-life, and it is shrinking. A person who stops learning does not stay in place while the world holds still; they fall behind as the field moves on without them. What looks like standing still is really sliding backward relative to everyone and everything that keeps moving. And because the field's movement compounds, so does the gap. A small distance opens at first, then widens, until catching up requires far more effort than keeping up ever would have.

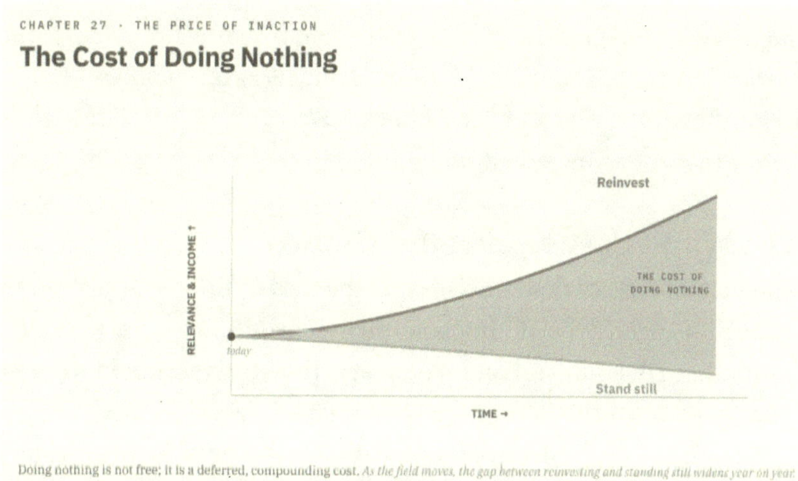

Figure 27.1 *The cost of doing nothing: the gap between reinvesting and standing still compounds over time.*

The widening gap in the figure is the heart of the matter. The cost of doing nothing is not a one-time penalty but a compounding one, and the longer the wait, the steeper the climb back. Acting early is cheap precisely because the gap is still small; acting late is expensive precisely because it is not.

The Slow Costs

Some of inaction's costs are quiet and cumulative. Income growth slows, as raises and opportunities flow toward those whose skills are current. Options narrow, as the interesting work goes to people who can do the new things. And a kind of stagnation sets in, the dull sense of a career that has stopped going anywhere. None of these is a catastrophe on any given day, which is exactly why they are so easy to tolerate and so costly to accumulate. They are the interest charges on a debt that never appears on a statement.

The Hidden Costs

Other costs are felt rather than counted. Chief among them is insecurity: the low-grade, persistent anxiety of suspecting that one's skills are slipping, that one is becoming replaceable, that the ground is moving and one is not. This stress is corrosive precisely because it is vague and ever-present, a background hum that action would quiet. Curiously, the discomfort of reinventing is often smaller than the discomfort of the anxiety it removes. Doing the work tends to feel better than worrying about not doing it.

The Worst Cost: Losing the Timing

The largest cost of doing nothing is the loss of timing. A person who reinvents early does it on their own schedule, from a position of strength, with a job and an income and time to experiment. A person who waits until they are forced, by a layoff, a restructure, a sudden obsolescence, reinvents from a position of weakness, in a hurry, under financial pressure, competing with everyone else who was caught out at the same moment. The work is the same; the conditions are far harsher. Acting early does not just reduce the cost of reinvention. It buys the priceless option of choosing when and how it happens.

This is why the timing, more than the effort, is what separates a calm reinvention from a frightening one. The person who begins while secure can experiment, fail cheaply, and choose a direction with a clear head. The person who begins in crisis has none of those luxuries: every decision carries the weight of rent and bills, and fear is a poor advisor. The early mover and the late mover do the same work, but one does it as an investor and the other as a casualty.

Inaction Is a Choice

All of this reframes doing nothing. It is not a neutral default, a safe place to stand while deciding. It is itself a decision, with its own mounting costs, made by not deciding. Seen clearly, the choice is not between the cost of action and no cost at all, but between two costs: the visible, controllable, front-loaded cost of acting, and the invisible, uncontrollable, compounding cost of not. Put that way, the investment the rest of this part describes starts to look less like a cost and more like the cheaper of two unavoidable bills.

If doing nothing is the expensive option, the sensible questions become how much to invest, and in what. The next chapters take them in turn, beginning with the currency that matters most and that everyone, regardless of budget, possesses: time.

IN PRACTICE

A B2B sales representative watched colleagues start using AI tools to research accounts, draft outreach, and prepare for calls, and decided it was a fad he could safely ignore. He was good at his job, his numbers were fine, and learning new tools felt like a distraction from selling. For a while, nothing happened, which only confirmed his choice.

Two years later, the distance had become hard to miss. The colleagues who had adopted early were covering more accounts, preparing faster, and closing more, while his own steady numbers now looked merely average against a rising bar. The raises and the best territories went to them. Catching up now meant learning under pressure what he could have learned at leisure, while his standing slipped. The cost of doing nothing had never sent him a bill, but he was paying it all the same, with interest, and from a weaker position than if he had started when the choice was still calm and his own.

IN SHORT

- Doing nothing feels free, but its cost is real, usually larger than the cost of acting, and deferred until it is hard to pay.
- Skills decay as the field moves; standing still is really sliding backward, and the gap compounds over time.
- The slow costs are quiet and cumulative: slower income growth, narrowing options, and stagnation.
- The hidden costs are felt rather than counted: the corrosive, low-grade insecurity of becoming replaceable.
- The worst cost is losing the timing: those who wait reinvent from weakness, on someone else's schedule, rather than from strength on their own.

ASK YOURSELF

1. What is the real, compounding cost of continuing to do nothing, made honest rather than left vague?
2. Where has standing still already turned into sliding backward relative to a moving field?
3. How much of the current background stress is the unpaid interest on deferred reinvention?
4. Would it be better to reinvent now, on one's own terms, or later, when forced and from a weaker position?

CHAPTER TWENTY-EIGHT
How Much Time Should You Invest?

The currency of reinvention is mostly time, not money. Almost everything that matters, learning the tools, building the stack, running the loop, is paid for in hours of attention rather than dollars. The practical question, then, is how many hours, and arranged how. The answer is less than most people fear, provided it is spent consistently rather than heroically.

Time Is the Real Currency

It is comforting to believe that reinvention requires a large budget, because that makes inaction someone else's fault: there was no money for it. The truth is less convenient. The binding constraint is almost never money; it is time and the consistent use of it. This is good news, because while budgets vary enormously between people, everyone has some hours, and the amount required is smaller than the dramatic version of reinvention suggests. The task is not to find vast stretches of time but to commit a modest amount, reliably.

Reframing time as the currency also clarifies where it has been going. Most people do not lack five hours so much as spend them elsewhere without noticing, on scrolling, on low-value busywork, on tasks that could be dropped. The audit from an earlier chapter applies to time as much as to tasks: found honestly, the hours for reinvention usually already exist, hidden inside a week that feels full but is not, on close inspection, full of the right things.

The Five-Hour Weekly Sprint

A sustainable baseline is about five hours a week. That is roughly an hour on most days, or a single focused block at the weekend, and it is enough to make real progress if it is genuinely consistent. The emphasis belongs on sustainable. The common pattern, a frantic burst of forty hours in one inspired week followed by months of nothing, accomplishes far less than five quiet hours sustained across a year. As an earlier chapter put it, consistency over months beats intensity over days. The five-hour week is the engine; everything larger is built from it.

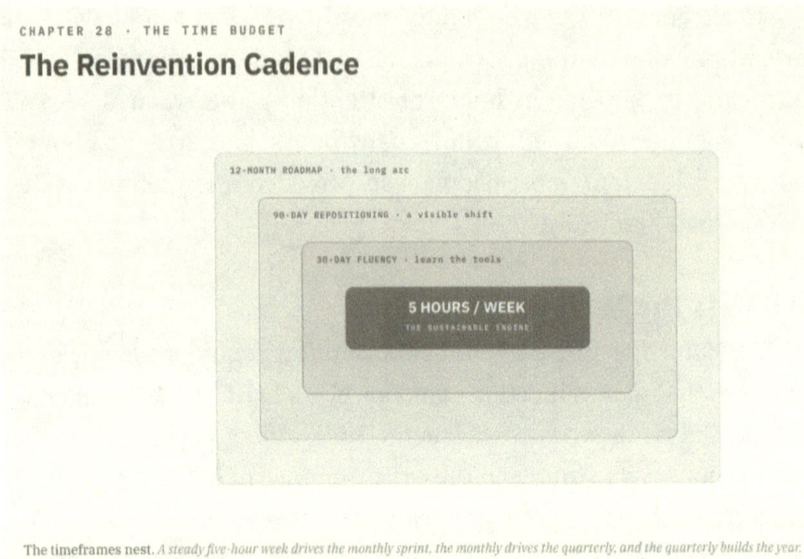

Figure 28.1 *The reinvention cadence: nested timeframes built on a sustainable weekly habit.*

What makes five hours enough is that the timeframes nest, as the figure shows. The weekly sprint is not an isolated effort but the smallest unit of a larger structure, feeding a monthly sprint, which feeds a quarterly one, which builds toward a yearly arc. Each scale serves a different purpose, and together they turn a modest weekly habit into substantial change over time.

The 30-Day Fluency Sprint

The first natural unit above the week is a month, and the first month is best spent reaching basic fluency. A 30-day fluency sprint has a single, focused goal: to become genuinely comfortable with the core AI tools relevant to one's field, past the awkward beginner stage and into practical, daily use. A month of consistent, deliberate practice is enough to cross that threshold, and the fluency it builds is the foundation everything else depends on. Trying to reposition a career before reaching basic fluency is building on sand.

Fluency, importantly, is not expertise. The goal of the first month is not mastery but comfort: enough familiarity to reach for the tools by instinct rather than avoiding them, to know roughly what they can and cannot do, and to use them in the ordinary course of work. That modest threshold is what unlocks everything after it, because a person who is merely curious about the tools behaves very differently from one who actually reaches for them, and only the second is positioned to reposition.

The 90-Day Repositioning Sprint

A quarter is long enough to make a visible shift. Where the month builds fluency, the 90-day sprint uses it to reposition: to complete a real project, build a meaningful new skill, redesign a workflow, or produce a piece of proof. Ninety days is a well-known unit for a reason. It is short enough to stay urgent and long enough to achieve something substantial, and a single focused quarter can move a person's standing in a way that a year of vague intention never would. The repositioning sprint is where the work becomes visible to others.

The 12-Month Roadmap

The outermost frame is the year. A 12-month roadmap holds the longer ambition, where a person wants to stand a year out, and breaks it into the quarters and months that will get there. Its job is direction, not detail. The roadmap keeps the weekly hours pointed at something larger than themselves, so that the small, consistent efforts accumulate toward a chosen destination rather than scattering. It is loose by design, because the loop will revise it, but without it the weekly sprint risks becoming busywork without a heading.

Why the Cadence Works

The power of the cadence is in the nesting. Any single timeframe alone falls short: a weekly habit without a yearly direction wanders, and a yearly plan without a weekly habit never starts. Linked together, they cover each other's weaknesses. The week supplies consistency, the month supplies focus, the quarter supplies visible progress, and the year supplies direction. Five hours, spent inside that structure, compounds into the kind of change that looks, from the outside, like a dramatic reinvention but was in fact a steady accumulation.

There is also a psychological reason the cadence works. Long-term goals are motivating in the abstract and paralysing in practice, because the distance between here and there is too large to act on. Nesting the timeframes shrinks that distance to something a person can hold: this week's five hours, this month's single focus. The year takes care of itself when the weeks are tended, and the structure quietly removes the overwhelm that stops most reinventions before they start.

Time, then, is the main investment, and a modest, well-structured amount of it is enough. Money is the smaller question, but it is not nothing, and spending it wisely, or wasting it, makes a real difference. That is the subject of the next chapter.

IN PRACTICE

An HR generalist wanted to reinvent herself for an AI-shaped profession but could not see where the time would come from. Her days were full, and the dramatic image of reinvention, evenings and weekends swallowed by study for months, was so daunting that she kept not starting at all.

What unlocked it was shrinking the commitment. She gave it five hours a week, an hour before work most days and nothing more, refusing to let it expand into burnout. The first month she spent simply reaching fluency with the tools her field was adopting. The next quarter she used that fluency to redesign her team's hiring workflow, a visible, concrete win. A year on, the modest weekly habit had compounded into a genuine repositioning, and the change that looked dramatic from the outside had been built five quiet hours at a time.

IN SHORT

- The main currency of reinvention is time, not money, and the amount required is smaller than the dramatic version suggests.
- About five hours a week, spent consistently, is a sustainable baseline; consistency beats intensity.
- The first 30 days are best spent reaching basic fluency with the relevant tools.
- A 90-day sprint is long enough to make a visible shift: a project, a skill, a redesigned workflow, or a piece of proof.
- The timeframes nest, the week feeding the month, the month the quarter, the quarter the year, turning a modest habit into substantial change.

ASK YOURSELF

1. Where could five consistent hours a week come from, without expanding into burnout?
2. What would a focused 30-day push toward basic fluency with the relevant tools look like?
3. What single visible shift could a 90-day sprint realistically produce?
4. What is the one-year destination, and what quarters and months would lead to it?

CHAPTER TWENTY-NINE

How Much Money Should You Invest?

If time is the main currency of reinvention, money is the secondary one, and it matters far less than the marketing around it suggests. A great deal can be accomplished for nothing, and a great deal of money can be spent accomplishing nothing. Spending well is less about how much and more about what, and when, and the difference between an investment and a waste is usually a matter of timing and honesty.

Less Than It Seems

The barrier to reinvention is rarely the price of entry. The most important tools have capable free versions, the knowledge needed is largely available at no cost, and the communities worth joining are often free to enter. The image of reinvention as an expensive undertaking, requiring costly courses and certifications, is mostly a story told by the people selling them. For most of the journey, the right budget is close to zero, and treating money as the obstacle is usually a way of avoiding the real obstacle, which is time and effort.

This is worth stating plainly because the opposite belief is so common and so convenient. Believing reinvention requires money makes its absence forgivable, a matter of circumstance rather than choice. But the people who adapt fastest are rarely those who spent the most; they are those who started with what was free, used it seriously, and paid only for the few things that genuinely accelerated them. Cost is almost never the real barrier, and treating it as one is usually a polite way of not beginning.

Start Free

The sensible default is to start free and stay free until paying clearly buys something free cannot. The foundation of fluency can be built entirely at no cost: the free tiers of the major tools, the abundant free documentation and tutorials, and communities where people share what works. A person who exhausts the free options before spending anything will have both learned a great deal and developed the judgment to know what, if anything, is actually worth paying for.

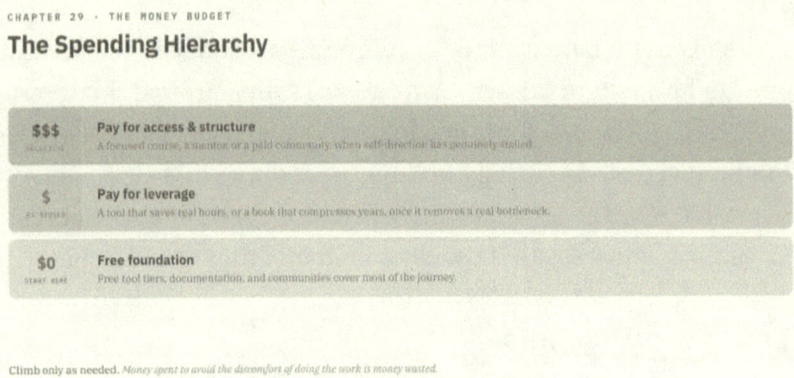

Figure 29.1 *The spending hierarchy: build on the free foundation and pay upward only as needed.*

The hierarchy in the figure is a guide to climbing only as needed. The free foundation comes first and covers most of the ground. Paid leverage comes next, but only when it removes a real bottleneck. And the higher spending, on access and structure, comes last, reserved for the specific moments it is genuinely warranted. The order matters: spending should follow need, not precede it.

When to Pay

There are three good reasons to spend money. The first is leverage: a paid tool that reliably saves real hours, or a book that compresses years of someone's experience into an afternoon, pays for itself quickly. The second is structure: when self-direction has genuinely failed, not merely faltered, a well-chosen course can supply the scaffolding to get moving again. The third is access: a mentor, a coach, or a paid community can shortcut months of trial and error by connecting a person to those who have already walked the path. In each case the test is the same: does the spending remove a real, identified bottleneck?

It helps to notice what these three reasons have in common. None of them is about acquiring information, which is now nearly free, and all of them are about removing a specific constraint: a slow task, a stalled will, a missing connection. Spending that targets a named bottleneck tends to pay off; spending that targets a vague unease tends not to. Before any purchase, the useful question is simply which bottleneck this removes, and whether that bottleneck is actually the thing currently in the way.

When Not to Spend

The most common waste is buying learning as a substitute for doing it. It is far more comfortable to purchase a course than to face the discomfort of practising, and so people accumulate courses, certifications, and subscriptions as a way of feeling productive without being so. This is procrastination wearing the costume of diligence. The unfinished course, the certificate collected for reassurance, the next program bought before the last was used: these are not investments but avoidance. Money spent to feel like one is reinventing, rather than to actually reinvent, is simply gone.

The deeper trap is that buying feels like progress while demanding none of the discomfort that real progress requires. Reading about a skill, or owning the course that teaches it, produces a pleasant sensation of advancement without the friction of practice, and that sensation is both addictive and false. The clearest sign of this pattern is a growing library of unfinished material alongside unchanged ability. The cure is not more buying but more doing, ideally with what is already owned or free.

Mentors and Communities

Among the things worth paying for, people are often the highest return. A mentor who has done what a person is attempting can compress the learning dramatically, steering them past the mistakes that would otherwise cost months. A good community provides the same benefit at lower intensity: a steady supply of what is working, what is not, and what is coming. These spends tend to repay themselves many times over, because what they buy is not information, which is cheap, but judgment and direction, which are not.

Money, spent on the right things at the right time, accelerates reinvention; spent on the wrong things, it merely soothes. Either way, the spending is only justified by what it returns. Which raises the final and most important question of this part: how to tell whether any of this investment, of time or money, is actually paying off.

IN PRACTICE

A freelance video editor, anxious about AI, did what anxious people often do: he spent money. He bought several expensive courses, a stack of subscriptions, and a premium certification, and felt, briefly, that he was taking action. Months later, most of the courses sat unfinished, the certification had changed nothing, and his actual skills were where they had started.

When the spending stopped, the learning began. He started with the free tiers of the tools and the abundant free tutorials, and forced himself to use them on real client projects rather than buying more instruction. The only money that paid off was small and specific: one tool subscription that genuinely saved him hours, and a modest community of editors a step ahead of him. He had learned the hard way that money spent to avoid the discomfort of doing the work is wasted, and that the cheapest path was also the one that actually worked.

IN SHORT

- Money matters far less than marketing suggests; much can be done for nothing, and much money can be spent achieving nothing.
- Start free and stay free until paying clearly buys something the free options cannot.

- Pay for three things: leverage that saves real hours, structure when self-direction has genuinely failed, and access to people further ahead.
- The common waste is buying courses and certificates as a substitute for the discomfort of actually doing the work.
- Mentors and communities are often the highest-return spend, because they buy judgment and direction rather than mere information.

ASK YOURSELF

1. Have the free options genuinely been exhausted before any money was spent?
2. Of recent or planned spending, what removes a real bottleneck, and what merely soothes anxiety?
3. Where might buying a course be standing in for the harder work of practising?
4. Who, as a mentor or community, could shortcut months of trial and error?

CHAPTER THIRTY

How to Measure Return on Reinvention

Time and money have been invested. The natural next question is whether the investment is working. Reinvention is too often run on faith, a vague hope that the effort will pay off someday, and faith is hard to sustain and easy to misdirect. The remedy is to treat each cycle of reinvention as what it is, an investment with a measurable return, and to actually look at the return. This is the idea of Return on Reinvention.

Reinvention as Investment

Return on Reinvention, or RoR, is a simple frame: the returns a cycle produces, set against the time and money it cost. Stated as a ratio, it turns a hazy sense of progress into something that can be examined and steered. The point is not to compute a precise figure, which is neither possible nor necessary, but to ask, honestly and regularly, whether the investment is producing a return worth the cost, and which investments are producing the most.

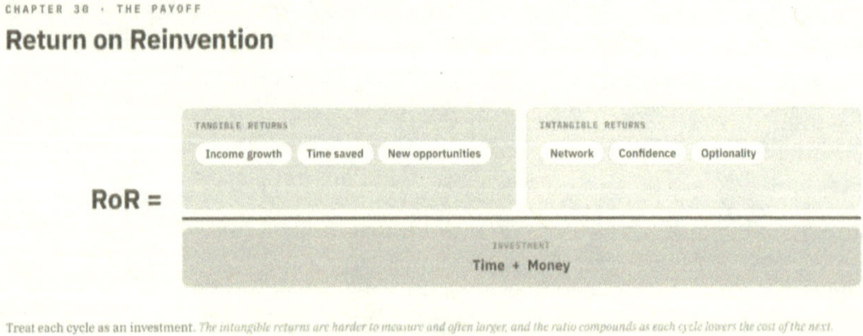

Figure 30.1 *Return on Reinvention: the returns of a cycle set against the time and money it cost.*

The figure lays the idea out plainly. On top sit the returns, both the tangible kind that can be counted and the intangible kind that can only be felt; underneath sits the investment of time and money. A high return means a cycle gave back a great deal for what it cost; a low one is a signal to change approach. Measuring is what converts reinvention from an act of faith into a process with feedback.

It is worth being clear about what measuring is not. It is not an exercise in spreadsheets and false precision, assigning dubious numbers to things that resist them. It is closer to the retrospective from an earlier chapter: a regular, honest look at whether the effort is repaying itself, and where the best returns are coming from. The aim is direction, not decimal places, and even a rough sense of the return is enough to steer by, which is all steering ever requires.

The Tangible Returns

Some returns can be counted directly. Income growth is the most obvious: raises, higher-paying roles, better-paid clients, the market's response to rising capability. Time saved is another, the hours reclaimed when a tool or skill makes the work faster, hours that can be reinvested in the next cycle. And new opportunities are a third: the roles, projects, and clients that become available only because a person can now do something they could not before. These are the returns that show up in a bank balance or a calendar, and they are the easiest to point to.

These countable returns are useful precisely because they are concrete, but they are also lagging: income and opportunities often arrive well after the capability that earns them. A person who judges reinvention only by its immediate financial return will frequently conclude, too early, that it is not working, and stop just before it pays. The tangible returns are real and worth tracking, but they are the slowest to appear, which is exactly why the intangible ones matter so much in the meantime.

A simple way to keep the countable returns in perspective is to track them over quarters rather than weeks. A single month may show nothing, while a year shows a clear line, and the longer view prevents the premature conclusion that the effort has failed. The tangible returns are best read the way an investor reads a portfolio: not by staring at it daily, but by checking, at sensible intervals, whether the overall direction is upward.

The Intangible Returns

The larger returns are often the ones that resist counting. A network grows with each cycle, as reinvention brings a person into contact with others doing the same, and relationships compound in value over time. Confidence grows too, the quiet, durable security of knowing one can learn the next thing, which is worth more than any single skill. And optionality grows, the accumulating set of paths a person could take, each one a hedge against the others. These intangible returns are harder to measure and easy to dismiss, but over a career they often dwarf the tangible ones.

Of the three, optionality may be the most undervalued, because its payoff is invisible until it is suddenly essential. Each new capability, relationship, or asset is a door that need not be opened to be worth having; its value is the freedom it confers, the knowledge that if one path closes, others remain available. In a disrupted world, that freedom is a form of wealth in itself, and it accrues quietly to the person who keeps running the loop long after the immediate income gains have been banked.

The intangible returns also tend to arrive earlier than the tangible ones, which makes them useful as leading indicators. Confidence, a widening network, and a growing sense of options usually show up well before the raise or the new role does, and they signal that the tangible returns are on their way. A person who notices these early signs can keep faith with a cycle through the lag, trusting that the countable payoff is forming beneath the surface even when the bank balance has not yet moved.

Measuring to Steer

The purpose of measuring is not judgment but navigation. By looking honestly at which cycles returned the most, a person learns where to point the next ones: doubling down on the activities with a high return and quietly dropping those that returned little. This is the empirical spirit of the whole loop applied to the loop itself, letting evidence, not assumption, decide where the effort goes. A reinvention that is measured is a reinvention that improves, because each cycle informs the next.

Honest measurement does require resisting two temptations. The first is to count only what is easy, the income and the hours, and to ignore the network, confidence, and optionality that may matter more. The second is to demand returns too quickly, abandoning a cycle before its slower payoffs have had time to arrive. Good measurement holds both in view: it credits the intangible alongside the tangible, and it judges a cycle on a horizon long enough for the real return to show.

In practice, the measurement can be as light as a few lines in a notebook at the end of each cycle: what was invested, what came back, and what to do more or less of next time. The discipline is in doing it at all, not in doing it elaborately. Most people never measure their reinvention in any form, which is precisely why so many abandon it, unable to see the returns that were quietly accumulating the whole time.

The Compounding Return

The most important feature of Return on Reinvention is that it compounds. The returns of one cycle, a stronger skill, a wider network, more confidence, a tool that saves time, lower the cost and raise the return of the next. The first cycle is the hardest and least profitable; each subsequent one is cheaper and pays more, as the foundation built earlier does some of the work. Reinvention is not a flat tax paid over and over but an investment that, run consistently, becomes more rewarding the longer it runs.

Compounding also explains why early discouragement is so misleading. The first cycle, judged on its own, can look like a poor trade: much effort, little visible return. But that cycle is buying the foundation, the fluency, the first relationships, the initial confidence, on which every later cycle earns more. Quitting after the first is like abandoning an investment in the year it was made, just before the returns begin to build on themselves. The loop rewards patience precisely because its best returns are back-loaded.

Seen across years rather than weeks, this is perhaps the most encouraging fact in the whole book. The person who keeps running the loop is not paying an ever-rising tax to stay afloat; they are making an investment that grows easier and more rewarding with time, as skills, relationships, confidence, and options accumulate into a base that does much of the work. Disruption does not relent, but neither does the compounding, and the compounding is on the side of whoever keeps going.

This completes the economics of reinvention: the cost of doing nothing, the time to invest, the money to spend, and the return to expect. Understanding the numbers, though, is not the same as having a plan. The final move is to turn all of it, the why, the what, the when, the where, the how, and the how much, into a concrete, time-boxed plan of action. That is the work of Part Eight: the ESCAPE Plan.

IN PRACTICE

A UX researcher had been reinventing herself diligently for a year, taking courses and learning tools, but had no real sense of whether any of it was paying off. The effort felt virtuous but unmeasured, and without a sense of return she found her motivation flagging.

She began treating each cycle as an investment and asking what it returned. Some returns were easy to see: a new skill that had won her a better-paid contract, a tool that saved her several hours a week. Others were quieter but larger: a network that had grown through a community, a confidence that she could now learn whatever came next, and a set of options that no longer depended on a single employer. Seeing the returns let her steer, doubling down on what paid and dropping what did not, and noticing that each cycle cost less and returned more than the one before. The reinvention that had felt like an act of faith became a process she could measure, and improve.

IN SHORT

- Treat each cycle of reinvention as an investment with a measurable return, rather than running it on faith.
- Return on Reinvention sets the returns of a cycle against the time and money it cost.
- Tangible returns can be counted: income growth, time saved, and new opportunities.
- Intangible returns resist counting but often dominate: a wider network, durable confidence, and growing optionality.
- Measuring lets a person steer, doubling down on high-return activities, and the return compounds as each cycle lowers the cost of the next.

ASK YOURSELF

1. For a recent reinvention cycle, what did it actually return against what it cost?
2. Which returns are tangible and countable, and which are intangible but possibly larger?
3. Which past efforts had a high return worth repeating, and which had little worth dropping?
4. How might the returns of earlier cycles be lowering the cost of the next one?

PART EIGHT

THE PLAN

The 90-Day AI Disruption Escape Roadmap

Everything so far becomes a plan: ninety days, five phases, and a few hours a week, turning the why, the what, the when, the where, the how, and the how much into action.

CHAPTER THIRTY-ONE

Set Up Your Board (Day 0)

Every part of this book until now has been preparation. The why, the what, the when, the where, the how, and the how much all point toward a single thing: a concrete plan, run over ninety days, that turns understanding into change. This part is that plan. It begins not with action but with setup, on what can be called Day Zero, because a plan without a system to carry it is just another good intention waiting to dissolve.

The Plan Begins With Infrastructure

It is tempting to start a ninety-day plan by doing something immediately, but the first move is to build the structure that will hold the next ninety days together. That structure is the reinvention board from an earlier chapter, set up properly before the clock starts. The half-hour spent building it is the highest-leverage time in the whole plan, because it is what converts a burst of motivation into a system that keeps running after the motivation fades.

Define the Vision

The board begins with a vision: a single sentence describing the person worth becoming over the coming months. It is not a detailed plan and not a job title, but a direction, something like becoming the person on the team who turns AI into real results. The vision's job is to give every later decision a reference point, so that when a choice arises about what to learn or build, there is a clear standard against which to judge it.

Build the Backlog

Beneath the vision sits the backlog: a single list capturing everything worth trying. Skills to learn, tools to test, experiments to run, outcomes to produce, all of it goes here, without any commitment to doing all of it. The backlog is a place to empty the head, so that good ideas are captured rather than lost and the mind is freed from holding them. Most of it will wait, and some of it will never be done, and that is exactly how a backlog is supposed to work.

A good backlog also lowers the anxiety that fuels paralysis. Much of the dread around reinvention comes from the sense of a vast, undefined task looming with no clear edges. Writing it all down gives it edges. The mountain becomes a list, the list becomes cards, and the cards become a single next thing to do this week. Capture, it turns out, is calming, because a worry written into a backlog stops circling the mind and waits, quietly, for its turn.

The Board

The vision and backlog become a working board with three simple columns: the backlog itself, the one sprint active right now, and the work already done.

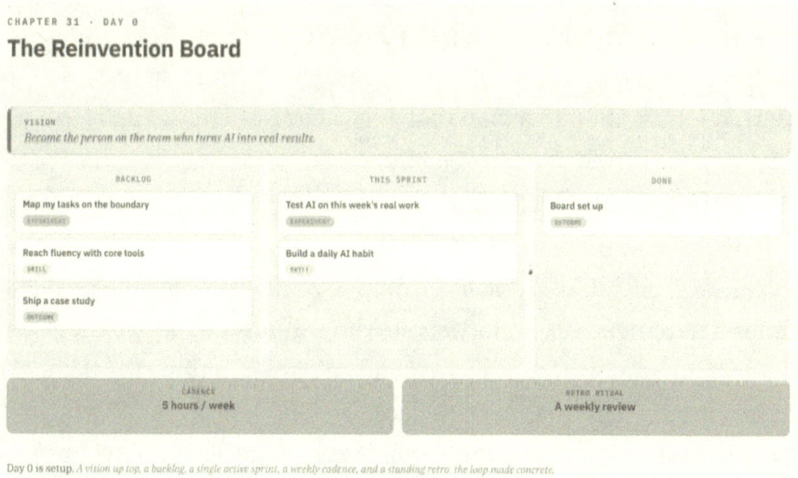

Figure 31.1 *The reinvention board: a vision, a backlog, one active sprint, a cadence, and a retro ritual.*

The cards moving across it are the substance of the plan, tagged as skills, experiments, or outcomes so their nature is clear at a glance. The rule is that only a small number of cards occupy the active sprint at once, which protects focus and prevents the board from becoming a wish list nothing ever leaves. A card that reaches done is a small, visible proof that the plan is moving.

Choose the Cadence

The board runs on a cadence, and the sustainable one established earlier is about five hours a week. Those hours are chosen, blocked, and protected in advance, not left to whatever time happens to remain, because time that is not protected is time that disappears. Work is pulled into the sprint as capacity allows rather than pushed on an unrealistic schedule, which keeps the pace honest and the plan alive past the first enthusiastic fortnight.

Set the Retro Ritual

The last piece of the setup is a standing ritual: a short weekly review, a retro, scheduled like any other commitment. Its purpose is to inspect and adapt, to ask what worked, what did not, and what to change, so that the plan improves itself as it runs. Without this ritual, a plan drifts; with it, every week is a small course correction, and ninety days of small corrections add up to a plan that gets steadily better at delivering.

Why Day Zero Matters

All of this can be built in well under an hour, which makes it easy to dismiss as trivial. It is not. The setup is what separates the people who intend to reinvent from the people who actually do, because it gives the intention somewhere to live and a next action to take. Most reinventions fail not from a lack of will but from a lack of this scaffolding, and an hour spent building it is the cheapest insurance the whole plan offers.

There is a reason the setup works where willpower fails. Willpower is a finite resource that fades under stress and busyness, while a system runs on its own momentum, asking only that the next card be picked up. By placing the plan onto a board, a person stops relying on memory and motivation and starts relying on structure, which is far more durable. The hour of setup, in effect, buys a substitute for the discipline that no one can summon reliably for ninety straight days.

With the board built, the vision set, the cadence protected, and the retro scheduled, the system is ready. The ninety days can begin, and they begin where all reinvention begins: with seeing the work clearly. The first fortnight is for mapping.

IN PRACTICE

A marketing coordinator had read widely about AI and reinvention and felt thoroughly convinced and entirely stuck. She knew she needed to change, agreed with every argument for it, and yet weeks passed with nothing done, the intention dissolving into a busy calendar.

On a quiet Sunday she spent an hour on Day Zero. She wrote a one-line vision, emptied her head of every skill and experiment worth trying into a backlog, pulled two cards into a first sprint, and blocked five hours across the coming week. She set a Friday review on her calendar. Nothing about the work had changed, but everything about her relationship to it had: the vague, paralysing resolve was now a small, concrete system with a next action. The board did what conviction alone never had, which was to make her actually begin.

IN SHORT

- Day Zero is setup: before the ninety days begin, build the system that will carry them.
- Define a one-line vision, a direction to aim at rather than a detailed plan.
- Fill a backlog with every skill, experiment, and outcome worth trying, without committing to all of it.

- Set up a simple board with backlog, this-sprint, and done columns, and tag the cards.
- Choose a sustainable cadence of about five hours a week, and a standing weekly retro ritual.

ASK YOURSELF

1. What single sentence captures the vision, the person worth becoming over the next ninety days?
2. What belongs in the backlog right now: which skills, experiments, and outcomes are worth trying?
3. Where will the weekly five hours actually come from, and how will they be protected?
4. When, each week, will the retro happen, and what will it review?

CHAPTER THIRTY-TWO

Days 1-15: Awareness and Exposure Mapping

The first two weeks of the plan are not for doing but for seeing. It is a strong temptation to rush straight into learning tools and building things, but reinvention built on a guess about where the exposure lies tends to aim at the wrong targets. The first fortnight is spent mapping: understanding the real work, testing where AI actually stands against it, and noticing the early signs of where things are heading.

Start by Seeing

This is the Expose step of the loop, given a fixed two-week window. The aim is a clear, honest picture of the work as it really is, not as the job description claims or as pride would prefer. Everything that follows, the fluency built, the value created, the repositioning made, depends on the accuracy of this picture, which is why it earns two full weeks rather than a rushed afternoon. A map drawn carelessly sends every later step in the wrong direction.

Map the Work as a System

The mapping begins by listing the real tasks that fill an actual week, in detail, and then seeing them not as a list but as a system: inputs, steps, handoffs, and outputs. Most people have never looked at their own work this closely, and the act of doing so is itself revealing. It surfaces the tasks that quietly consume the most time, the steps that exist only out of habit, and the points where value is really created, all of which a vague sense of the job conceals.

It helps to write the tasks down over a real week rather than from memory, because memory flatters. Asked to describe a job, most people recall the interesting, high-value parts and forget the hours lost to routine. A live log of an actual week tells the truth, and the truth is usually that more time than expected goes to work that is repetitive, low-value, or quietly automatable. That gap between the remembered job and the real one is exactly what the mapping exists to close.

The Boundary Map

With the tasks listed, each one is placed on the boundary between human and machine work, a line that runs from the firmly human to the fully automatable.

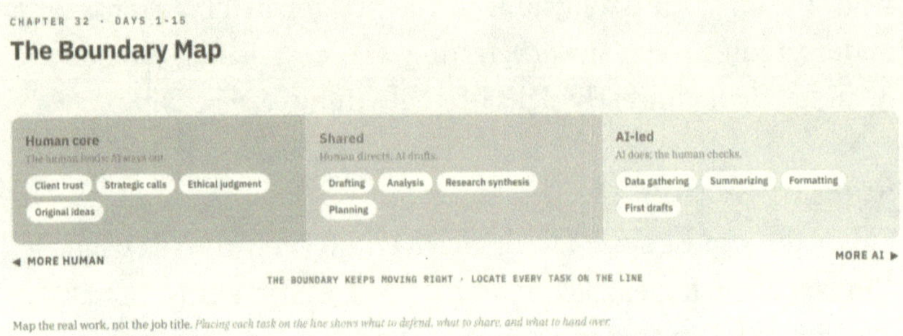

Figure 32.1 *The Boundary Map: locate every real task on the line between human and AI work.*

Some tasks fall in the human core, where judgment, trust, and originality keep them firmly on the human side. Others fall in the shared zone, where a human directs and the tool drafts. And others fall on the AI-led side, where the tool does the work and a person merely checks it. Placing every task on the line turns a vague anxiety about AI into a precise map of what to defend, what to share, and what to hand over.

Test AI Against Real Work

The boundary cannot be drawn from assumption; it has to be tested. The discipline of this fortnight is to take real tasks from a real week and actually run the current tools against them, rather than guessing where they stand. The results routinely surprise, in both directions: tools handle some work better than expected and stumble on things that looked easy. Only this empirical testing, evidence over ego once again, produces a map that can be trusted enough to plan on.

Find the Weak Signals

The final task of the fortnight is to look up from the present and notice the weak signals: the early, faint indicators of where the boundary is moving. Where are the tools improving fastest? Which tasks that are safe today look shaky on a two-year view? What are the most adaptive colleagues starting to do differently? These signals are quiet now and will be loud later, and catching them early is the difference between leading a shift and scrambling to catch up with it.

Weak signals are easy to dismiss precisely because they are weak; the whole skill is taking them seriously while they are still small. A tool that is clumsy today but improving quickly matters more than one that is capable today but static, because the trajectory counts for more than the snapshot. The fortnight's habit of looking for these signals, and noting them on the board, builds an early-warning sense that turns surprises into things merely seen coming.

By the end of fifteen days, the work is mapped, the boundary is drawn from evidence, and the direction of travel is visible. The map shows exactly where to aim. The next step is to build the capability to act on it, in a focused sprint toward fluency.

IN PRACTICE

A supply chain planner assumed he already knew which parts of his job were exposed to AI, and his assumptions were mostly wrong. When he finally sat down to map his real tasks rather than his job description, the picture surprised him.

He listed each task and placed it on the boundary. The forecasting he had thought was safely his turned out to sit squarely in the shared zone, better done with AI directing the number-crunching. The supplier relationships he had undervalued were firmly in the human core. And a stack of reporting he had never questioned belonged on the AI-led side entirely. Testing the tools against a real week, rather than guessing, corrected a map he had been navigating by for years, and the corrected map told him exactly where to aim the sprints that followed.

IN SHORT

- The first two weeks are for mapping, not doing: reinvention should rest on a clear picture, not a guess.
- Map the real tasks that fill a week, not the job description, and see them as a system.
- The Boundary Map places each task on the human-AI line: human core, shared, or AI-led.
- Test the tools against real work rather than assuming what they can do; let evidence decide.
- Watch for weak signals, the early signs of where the boundary is moving, which become strong trends later.

ASK YOURSELF

1. Listed honestly, what are the real tasks of a week, as opposed to the job description?
2. Placed on the Boundary Map, which tasks are human core, which shared, and which AI-led?
3. Which assumption about what AI can or cannot do has not actually been tested on real work?
4. What weak signals are already visible about where the boundary is heading?

CHAPTER THIRTY-THREE

Days 16-30: AI Fluency Sprint

The map from the first fortnight shows where to act; the second fortnight builds the ability to do so. This is the fluency sprint, a focused two weeks devoted to becoming genuinely comfortable with the AI tools that matter for the work. The goal is not mastery, which takes far longer, but fluency: enough practical skill to use the tools by instinct rather than avoiding them.

From Mapping to Doing

Where the first sprint was about seeing, this one is about capability. It marks the shift from understanding the problem to building the skill that addresses it, and it is the first place in the plan where visible, hands-on practice begins. The temptation here is to keep reading and researching, which feels productive but builds nothing. Fluency is a practical skill, and practical skills are built only by doing, repeatedly, with real work.

Pick the Core Tools

The sprint starts by choosing two or three tools, no more, that genuinely fit the work the map identified. The instinct to learn every available tool is a trap; it spreads attention so thin that nothing becomes second nature. Depth beats breadth here. A person fluent in two tools that matter is far better positioned than one who has dabbled in ten, and the few chosen tools should be the ones that touch the highest-value parts of the actual work.

Choosing the few tools well is itself an act of judgment, informed by the map. The right tools are the ones that sit on the high-value tasks, the work in the human core and the shared zone, rather than the ones that happen to be most talked about. A tool that speeds up trivial work is a poor use of a fluency sprint; a tool that strengthens the work that actually matters is worth the focused fortnight. The map drawn earlier is what makes this choice clear.

The Fluency Sprint

The fortnight follows a simple progression, from choosing the tools to wiring the first of them into a real piece of work.

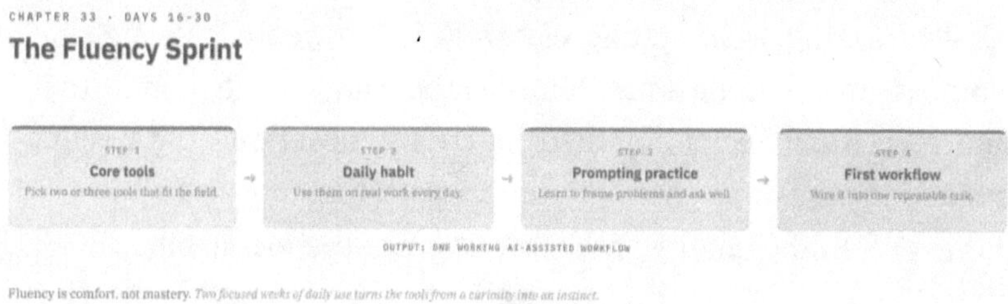

Figure 33.1 *The fluency sprint: from core tools and daily practice to one working AI-assisted workflow.*

It moves from selecting the core tools, to using them daily, to practising the framing and prompting that direct them well, to building a first workflow. Each step rests on the one before, and the whole progression is designed to end not with abstract knowledge but with a concrete, working result that proves the fluency is real.

Build a Daily AI Habit

The engine of the sprint is daily use. Rather than setting aside the tools for special study, the practice is to fold them into ordinary work every single day, so that fluency accumulates through repetition. A small amount of real use each day builds far more skill than an occasional long session, because the goal is to make reaching for the tools automatic, and only repetition makes anything automatic. By the end of two weeks, the awkwardness of the early attempts is gone.

Anchoring the habit to existing work makes it stick. Rather than carving out a separate slot for practice, the trick is to route real, already-scheduled tasks through the tools, so that the practice rides on work that was happening anyway. This removes the burden of finding extra time and ensures the fluency built is the kind that transfers, because it was developed on the genuine article rather than on exercises. Habits attached to real work survive; habits that depend on spare time rarely do.

Practise Prompting and Framing

Alongside daily use comes deliberate practice at prompting and problem framing, one of the layers of the advantage stack. This is the skill of asking well: stating clearly what is wanted, giving the right context, and shaping a problem so a tool can actually help with it. It is more art than recipe, learned by trying, observing the results, and adjusting. The difference between a frustrating tool and a powerful one is very often the quality of the framing, not the tool itself.

Ship the First Workflow

The sprint ends with a deliverable: one repeatable task, wired into a working AI-assisted workflow. This is the moment fluency becomes concrete, a real piece of the week now done faster or better with the tools as a genuine part of the process. The workflow need not be ambitious; it needs only to work, and to prove that the tools have crossed from curiosity into daily use. That single working workflow is the foundation the value sprint will build on.

With fluency built and a first workflow running, the internal capability is in place. The next month turns that capability outward, into value that other people can see, by improving one real process and proving the result.

IN PRACTICE

An executive assistant gave herself a two-week fluency sprint and resisted the urge to learn everything. She picked two tools that touched her actual work, scheduling and drafting, and committed to using them every day rather than reading about them.

By the end of the fortnight, the tools had stopped feeling foreign. She had developed a feel for what they did well and where they failed, learned to frame her requests so they were genuinely useful, and wired one of them into the weekly briefing she prepared, turning a half-day task into an hour. The fluency was modest, not mastery, but it was the threshold that mattered: she now reached for the tools by instinct, and that single working workflow was proof that the sprint had done its job.

IN SHORT

- The second fortnight builds fluency: the capability to act on what the map revealed.
- Pick two or three core tools that fit the field, and choose depth over breadth.
- Build a daily AI habit by using the tools on real work; fluency comes from repetition, not study.
- Practise prompting and problem framing, the skill of asking well and shaping a problem for the tool.
- Ship one AI-assisted workflow: a single repeatable task wired up, turning fluency into something concrete.

ASK YOURSELF

1 Which two or three tools genuinely fit the work and deserve a focused fortnight?

2 What would a daily AI habit, used on real tasks, look like in practice?

3 Where is prompting or problem framing currently the weak link, and how could it improve?

4 Which single repeatable task could become the first AI-assisted workflow?

CHAPTER THIRTY-FOUR

Days 31-60: Value Creation Sprint

Fluency is an internal achievement; on its own, it changes nothing that others can see. The third sprint, a full month, turns that fluency into visible value by taking one real process and making it measurably better. This is where reinvention stops being preparation and starts producing proof, and where the plan first creates something an employer or client would genuinely care about.

From Fluency to Value

The shift this month is from capability to contribution. It is entirely possible to be fluent with the tools and still deliver nothing visible, which is why the plan does not stop at fluency. The aim now is a concrete improvement to real work, the kind of result that shows up in outcomes rather than in a description of new skills. Value that others can see is what protects a career, and this sprint exists to create some.

Pick One Process

The sprint begins with a deliberate narrowing: choosing a single process to improve, rather than attempting to transform everything at once. The right choice is a process that is real, important, and currently painful, slow, manual, or inconsistent, so that improving it is genuinely felt. Focusing on one process is not a lack of ambition but the source of the result; effort spread across many improvements produces none worth pointing to, while effort concentrated on one produces proof.

Choosing the process well repays the effort spent choosing. The best candidate is one that is painful enough that its improvement is felt, visible enough that others notice, and bounded enough to be finished within the month. A process that is too large will not be done; one that is too trivial will not be noticed. The sweet spot is a real, irritating, contained piece of work whose improvement makes a difference the right people can see.

The Value Creation Sprint

The work of the month is to take that one process from its current state to a visibly better one, using the human-AI workflow built during the fluency sprint.

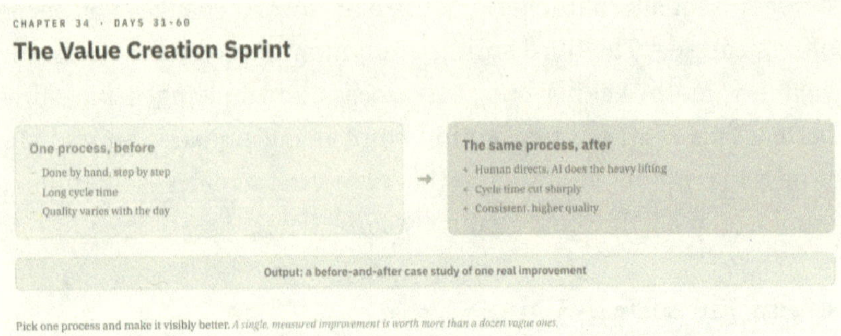

Figure 34.1 *The value creation sprint: rebuild one process and capture the before-and-after as proof.*

The redesign assigns the scale and drafting to the tools and keeps the judgment and decisions with the human, exactly as systems thinking prescribes. The result is a process that runs faster and produces better, more consistent output than before. The contrast between the before and the after is the point: it is what makes the value undeniable and, crucially, what makes it possible to prove.

Cut Cycle Time, Raise Quality

The twin targets of the redesign are speed and quality, and a well-designed human-AI workflow can usually improve both at once. Cutting the cycle time, the hours or days a process takes, frees capacity for the next cycle of reinvention. Raising the quality, the consistency and value of the output, makes the improvement matter to others. Pursuing both together, rather than trading one for the other, is what turns a modest tweak into a result worth a case study.

It is worth measuring both before and after, even roughly, because numbers are what make the improvement credible. A claim that a process is faster persuades no one; a note that it dropped from three days to half a day persuades almost everyone. The measurement need not be precise to the minute, but it must be honest and concrete, because the case study to come depends on it, and a before-and-after with real figures is far harder to wave away than an impression of progress.

Ship a Before-and-After Case Study

The deliverable of the month is proof: a short, honest before-and-after case study of the improvement, with real numbers attached. This is the Prove step of the loop made tangible. The case study captures what the process looked like before, what was changed, and what the result was, in terms others recognize as valuable. It is a small artifact with a large effect, because it converts invisible effort into a visible, portable record of value delivered.

One process, measurably improved and documented as proof, is a genuine win. The final month of the plan turns that single win into a repositioning, building the proof, the offer, and the portfolio that make the change durable.

IN PRACTICE

A procurement manager, newly fluent, was tempted to overhaul everything at once and wisely chose not to. Instead he picked a single process, the monthly supplier review, that was slow, manual, and quietly dreaded by everyone involved.

Over a month he rebuilt it as a human-AI workflow, with the tools gathering and summarizing the data and himself directing and deciding. The review that had taken three days now took half of one, and the analysis was sharper for it. He wrote the whole thing up as a short before-and-after case study, with the numbers attached, and circulated it. The single, measured improvement did more for his standing than any amount of general enthusiasm could have, precisely because it was concrete, visible, and his.

IN SHORT

- Month two turns internal fluency into value others can see, by improving one real process.
- Pick a single important process rather than trying to change everything at once.
- Rebuild it as a human-AI workflow to cut cycle time and raise quality at the same time.
- Capture the improvement as a before-and-after case study, with numbers, as proof of work.
- A single measured, visible win is worth more than scattered effort, because it is concrete and compounds trust.

ASK YOURSELF

1. Which one process, slow or frustrating, would be worth rebuilding as a human-AI workflow?
2. What would cutting its cycle time and raising its quality actually require?
3. How could the improvement be captured, with numbers, as a before-and-after case study?
4. Why might one measured, visible win matter more than a dozen vague improvements?

CHAPTER THIRTY-FIVE

Days 61-90: Reinvention Sprint

The final month gathers everything the plan has produced and turns it into a position. One improved process and one case study are a win, but a win is not yet a reinvention. This sprint consolidates: it builds the proof, sharpens the offer, assembles the portfolio, and closes with the retrospective that turns ninety days of effort into the first turn of a loop that will keep running.

From a Win to a Position

The instinct at this stage is to treat the case study as a finish line and stop. The more valuable move is to treat it as a foundation. A single visible win demonstrates capability; a reinvention establishes a new position, a changed sense of what a person does and what they are worth. This month is about that consolidation, taking the raw material of the previous sprints and shaping it into a coherent, defensible standing rather than a one-off result.

Build Proof of Work

The first task is to assemble the proof. The case study from the value sprint is the centrepiece, but around it can be gathered the other evidence the ninety days produced: the workflows built, the before-and-after results, the concrete examples of value delivered. Together these form a body of proof of work, a documented pattern rather than a single claim. Proof assembled deliberately is far more persuasive than proof scattered and half-remembered, and assembling it is the work of this stage.

Proof is most persuasive when it is specific. A general statement of competence invites doubt; a concrete record of a particular problem solved, with the situation, the action, and the result laid out, does not. The portfolio should favour the specific over the sweeping, a few real examples described plainly rather than a long list of skills claimed.

Specificity is what makes proof believable, and believable proof is what makes a repositioning land with the people who matter.

Create a New Offer

With the proof in hand, the next move is to articulate a new offer: a sharper statement of the value a person now provides. This is the repositioning made explicit, a shift from an old self-description to a new one, perhaps from someone who performs a task to someone who designs the AI-assisted system that performs it. The new offer can be floated internally, to a manager or team, or externally, to clients or a wider market, but it must be stated, because a repositioning no one hears about is not yet real.

The new offer does not require a dramatic announcement. Often it is conveyed simply by how a person now describes their work, the projects they volunteer for, and the problems they put themselves forward to solve. Over a few weeks, a consistent new framing reshapes how others see a role, especially when it is backed by the proof already assembled. The offer is less a single declaration than a steady, evidence-backed insistence on a changed value.

Build a Portfolio

The proof and the offer come together in a portfolio: a portable collection of evidence that travels with a person between roles and contexts. A portfolio is the beginning of optionality, the first asset in a career built on more than a single position. It need not be elaborate; it needs only to make the new capability and its results legible to others, so that the reinvention can be carried forward rather than left behind with a particular job.

A portfolio also changes how a person thinks about their own work, not only how others see it. Knowing that each project can become a documented piece of evidence quietly raises the standard of the work itself and turns ordinary tasks into potential proof. The habit of capturing outcomes, begun here, compounds over a career, so that years later a person has a rich record of capability to draw on rather than a thin list of job titles.

The Whole Arc

Standing at day ninety, it is worth looking back at the full shape of what the plan has done.

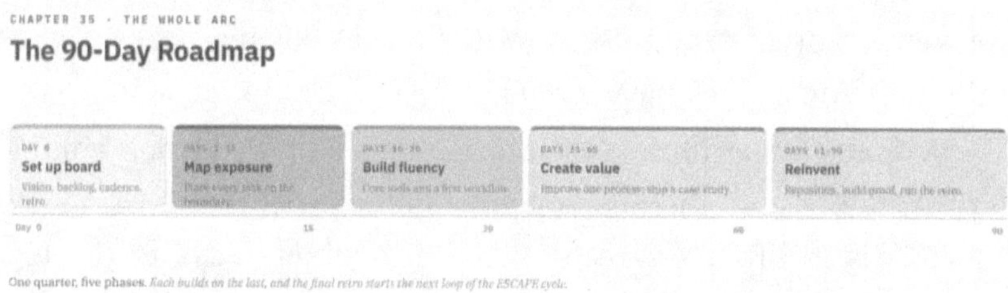

Figure 35.1 *The 90-day roadmap: five phases, each building on the last toward a repositioning.*

From the setup of Day Zero, through exposure mapping, the fluency sprint, the value sprint, and this final reinvention sprint, each phase rested on the one before. Ninety days that felt, from inside, like a series of small weekly efforts have produced, from outside, what looks like a substantial change. That is how reinvention actually works: not as a dramatic leap, but as a steady accumulation given structure.

Run the First Retro

The plan closes not with a celebration but with a retrospective. The same weekly ritual is run once more at full scale: an honest review of the whole ninety days, what worked, what did not, and what the next cycle should change. This is the inspect-and-adapt of the loop applied to the plan itself, and it is what makes the next ninety days better than the last. The retro is the hinge between one cycle and the next.

The Loop Continues

The most important thing the plan reveals is that it does not end. Ninety days is one turn of the ESCAPE Loop, not a finished destination, and the retrospective that closes it is also the audit that opens the next. There is no final, safe version of a career to arrive at, only a way of working that keeps producing safety as the ground keeps moving. The plan ends, deliberately, by beginning again.

Seen this way, the ninety-day plan is less a one-time project than a template that can be run again and again. The first time through is the hardest, because everything, the board, the cadence, the habits, is new. The second cycle starts from a running system and a foundation of proof, and so costs less and returns more, exactly as the economics of reinvention predicted. A person who finishes one plan has not merely reinvented once; they have learned how to reinvent on demand.

With the loop running, the practical work of the book is complete: a person now has a method, a plan, and the proof that it works. What remains is to lift the gaze from the next ninety days to the longer horizon, and to ask what kind of future this way of working is built for. That is the subject of the final part.

IN PRACTICE

A technical writer reached the final month of her ninety days with one solid case study and a decision to make: treat it as a finish line, or as a foundation. She chose foundation.

She spent the month turning a single win into a position. She gathered her proof into a small portfolio, sharpened how she described her value, from writer of documents to designer of AI-assisted documentation systems, and floated a new offer to her team and to a contact outside it. Then she ran a ninety-day retrospective, honestly noting what had worked and what to change. The plan had not delivered a final, finished version of her career; it had delivered a repositioning and, more importantly, a working loop she now knew how to run again. The last day of the plan was also the first day of the next one.

IN SHORT

- The final month turns one win into a repositioning: consolidate rather than treating the case study as a finish line.
- Build proof of work into a small, portable portfolio of evidence.
- Create a new offer: a sharper statement of value, a service, or a redefined role.
- A portfolio of proof is the start of optionality, something that travels between roles.
- Run a ninety-day retrospective; it does not end the work but starts the next turn of the ESCAPE Loop.

ASK YOURSELF

1 Is the instinct to treat the first win as a finish line, or as a foundation to build on?

2 What proof of work could be gathered into a small, portable portfolio?

3 How might the value now offered be described more sharply, or as a new offer entirely?

4 What would an honest ninety-day retrospective reveal, and what would the next loop change?

PART NINE

THE FUTURE

What Comes After Escaping AI Disruption?

Escaping disruption is not the end of the story but the start of a better one: leading with AI, leaning on what stays human, and running the loop for life.

CHAPTER THIRTY-SIX

From AI Survival to AI Leadership

Almost everything in this book so far has been about survival: how not to be left behind, made obsolete, or caught out by a change moving faster than most careers can. That framing was deliberate, because the threat is real and worth taking seriously. But it understates what running the loop actually produces. A person who audits, climbs, augments, proves, and evolves, again and again, does not merely stay afloat. They end up positioned to lead.

Beyond Survival

Survival is the floor of what the method delivers, not the ceiling. The same work that keeps a career safe, the honest audit, the built workflows, the visible proof, also accumulates into something more valuable: a person who genuinely understands how to turn AI into results, in a world where very few do. Scarcity creates value, and the ability to make AI useful, in real work, for real outcomes, is among the scarcest and most sought-after capabilities of the moment.

This reframing matters because it changes what the loop is for. Treated only as defence, reinvention is a grim necessity, a tax paid to avoid being discarded. Treated as a path to leadership, it becomes something a person might actually want to do, because the same effort that buys safety also buys influence, standing, and the satisfaction of shaping events rather than being shaped by them. The work is identical; the destination is far better than mere survival, and aiming for it costs nothing extra.

Three Stages

There is a natural progression in how a person relates to the technology, and it runs in three stages.

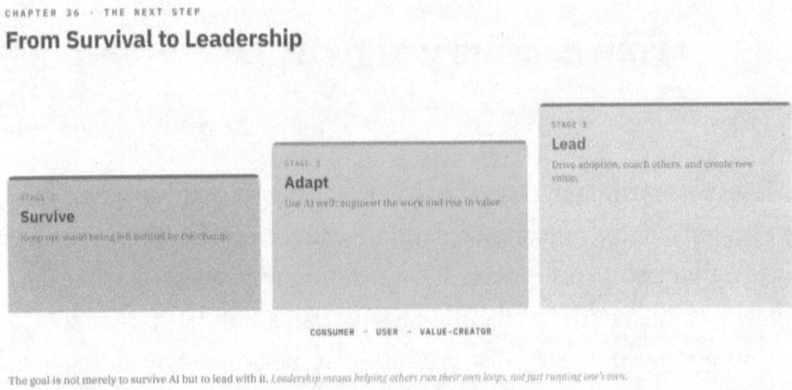

Figure 36.1 *From survival to leadership: the shift from keeping up, to using AI well, to leading with it.*

At first the relationship is about survival: keeping up, avoiding obsolescence, consuming the technology as it arrives. Then it becomes adaptation: using AI well, augmenting the work, rising in value as a capable user. And finally it becomes leadership: driving adoption, coaching others, and creating new value, as a person who shapes how the technology is used rather than merely reacting to it. The underlying shift is one of mindset, from consumer, to user, to value-creator.

Few people move through these stages by accident. Most stall at survival, doing just enough to keep up, because adapting and leading both demand a deliberate choice to engage rather than endure. The stages are less a ladder a person climbs automatically than a set of postures a person adopts, and the move from one to the next is a decision available at any time. Recognizing which stage one currently occupies is the first step toward choosing the next.

Lead the Adoption

A person who has run the loop is unusually well placed to lead AI adoption, because they have done the unglamorous work that most have only talked about. They have audited real tasks, tested tools against actual problems, designed human-AI workflows, and learned where the technology helps and where it fails. Organizations are desperate for exactly this kind of grounded, practical knowledge, and the person who possesses it is positioned to guide a team, a department, or an organization through a change it does not understand.

What makes this leadership credible is that it is earned rather than claimed. Anyone can advocate for AI in the abstract; very few can speak from the experience of having actually rebuilt their own work with it, with the scars and the specifics to prove it. That hard-won credibility is what organizations trust, and it cannot be faked or shortcut. The person who has quietly done the work carries an authority that no title or course confers, and it is exactly the authority a confused organization is looking for.

In practice, this often begins informally, long before any title changes. A colleague asks how a report got done so fast; a manager notices a workflow that used to take days; word spreads that a particular person seems to have figured the tools out. From there, leading the adoption is less a position to be appointed to than a role a person grows into by being visibly useful. The organization's need and the individual's readiness meet, and the leadership follows almost naturally.

Coach Others Through Their Loops

The highest-leverage move of all is to help others run their own loops. Teaching the method, the audit, the advantage stack, the systems thinking, the proof, multiplies a person's impact far beyond what they could achieve alone, and it builds something durable: influence, reputation, and the trust of people who were helped. A person who reinvents themselves earns safety; a person who helps a whole team reinvent earns a kind of standing that is very hard to take away.

There is a quiet selfishness in this generosity, in the best sense. Helping others reinvent does not diminish a person's own standing; it raises it, because a coach becomes the centre of a growing network of people who have reason to value them. In a world where so much is being automated, being the person others turn to when they need to adapt is among the most secure positions there is. Teaching the loop, it turns out, is one of the surest ways of strengthening one's own.

It also changes the emotional texture of the whole enterprise. Reinvention pursued alone, purely defensively, is a lonely and anxious business. Pursued in the open, in the service of helping others, it becomes something closer to a shared project, with allies rather than only competitors. The same loop that protects a single career can knit together a team that faces the change as a group, and a person who catalyses that is worth far more to an organization than one who merely keeps their own skills current.

The Value-Creator Mindset

What separates the leader from the survivor is finally a mindset. The survivor consumes AI to keep up; the user works with it to be productive; the value-creator asks a different question entirely, which is how the technology can be used to create something genuinely valuable for others. That orientation, toward creating value rather than merely avoiding harm, is what turns a defensive scramble into a position of strength, and it is available to anyone willing to adopt it.

The shift is subtle but transforming. A consumer asks what AI will do to them; a user asks what they can do with AI; a value-creator asks what they can do for others with it. Each question produces a different posture, and only the last leads anywhere worth going. The encouraging part is that the question is a choice, freely available regardless of role or seniority, and asking it differently is often the first concrete step from anxiety toward leadership.

Why Leadership Is the Safer Position

It can seem that aiming for leadership is riskier than simply trying to stay safe, but the opposite is true. Survivors react to change and remain vulnerable to the next one; leaders shape the change and accumulate the influence, relationships, and reputation that make them genuinely hard to replace. The most secure place to stand, it turns out, is not at the back of the room hoping to be overlooked, but at the front, helping everyone else find their way. Aiming higher is also aiming safer.

None of this requires a formal title or a position of authority. Leadership here is a matter of behaviour rather than rank: the person who runs the experiments, shares what works, and helps a colleague past a sticking point is leading, whatever their job description says. Influence of this kind is available to anyone willing to go first and bring others along, and it often precedes the formal recognition rather than waiting for it. The leading comes first; the title, if it matters, tends to follow.

Leadership, though, rests on a foundation, and it is worth being precise about what that foundation is. The thing that makes a person valuable as AI grows more capable is not their command of the tools, which others can also acquire, but something more durable and more human. That foundation is the subject of the next chapter.

IN PRACTICE

A nurse manager had spent two years quietly building her own AI fluency, mapping her unit's workflows, testing tools against the endless documentation that consumed her staff's time, and proving small improvements. She had, without quite naming it, run the loop. What she had not expected was where it left her.

When her hospital began a formal push to adopt AI, she was the obvious person to lead it, because she was the rare manager who had actually done the work rather than merely talking about it. She found herself coaching colleagues through the same audit and experiments she had run, helping each of them decide what to keep, what to automate, and what to protect. She had set out only to keep her own role safe and had arrived somewhere better: not surviving the change, but leading it, and pulling others along behind her.

IN SHORT

- Running the loop produces more than survival; it positions a person to lead the change rather than merely endure it.
- The progression runs from surviving, to adapting, to leading, and the mindset from consumer, to user, to value-creator.
- A person who has run the loop is well placed to lead AI adoption, having already done the audit and built the workflows.
- The highest-leverage move is coaching others through their own loops, which multiplies impact and builds influence.
- Leadership is the safer position, not the riskier one: leaders shape the change and are harder to replace than survivors.

ASK YOURSELF

1. On the path from surviving to leading, where does the current relationship with AI sit?
2. What AI adoption could be led, rather than merely waited for, in a current team or organization?
3. Who nearby could be coached through their own loop, and what would that take?
4. What would shifting from a consumer to a value-creator mindset actually change about the work?

CHAPTER THIRTY-SEVEN

The Human Advantage in an AI World

As AI grows more capable, a natural anxiety follows: if the machines can do more and more, what is left that is distinctly, valuably human? The answer is both reassuring and specific. A great deal is left, but it is not what many people instinctively try to defend. The human advantage does not lie in competing with AI at the things it does well. It lies in the opposite direction, in the capabilities that remain valuable precisely because the machines cannot reach them.

This is a more hopeful answer than the anxious question expects. It means the human advantage is not a shrinking remnant to be defended to the last, but a large and durable territory that the machines are, by their nature, unable to occupy. The task is not to find some small safe corner but to recognize how much of what matters most has always been human, and to move toward it deliberately as the merely mechanical work is handed off.

Stop Competing on AI's Terms

The losing strategy is to try to beat AI at its own game: to be faster, to recall more, to process at greater scale. These are the dimensions on which machines excel and humans cannot win, and a career staked on them is a career staked on a shrinking advantage. The winning strategy is to compete on human terms instead, to lean deliberately into the capabilities that do not reduce to speed, scale, or recall, and that grow more valuable, not less, as the machine-like work is automated away.

This is harder than it sounds, because the instinct under threat is to work faster and do more, to out-produce the very machines that out-produce effortlessly. That instinct leads straight into exhaustion and irrelevance. The counterintuitive move is to do less of what AI does well and more of what it cannot do at all, even though the second feels less productive in the moment. Competing on human terms means resisting the pull toward machine-like work and deliberately investing where the machine has no answer.

The Durable Human Core

There is a set of human capabilities that stays valuable by its very nature, a durable core that no advance in the tools erodes.

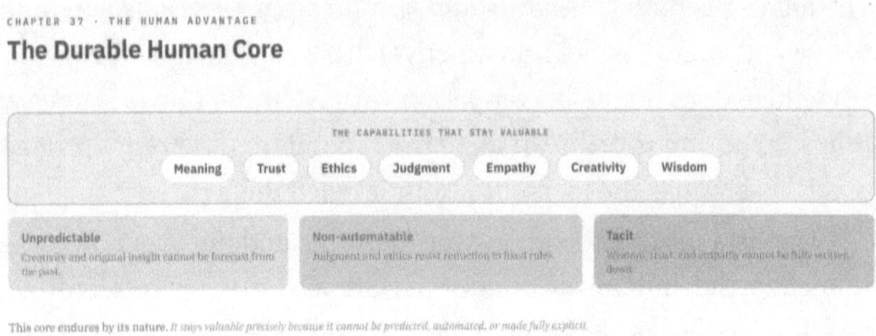

Figure 37.1 *The Durable Human Core: capabilities that endure because they cannot be predicted, automated, or made explicit.*

Meaning, trust, ethics, judgment, empathy, creativity, and wisdom share a quality that protects them. They are unpredictable, in that genuine creativity cannot be forecast from the past; non-automatable, in that judgment and ethics resist reduction to fixed rules; and tacit, in that wisdom, trust, and empathy cannot be fully written down. AI learns from patterns in what already exists, and these capabilities live exactly where the existing patterns run out.

It is worth noticing that these capabilities are not consolation prizes, the scraps left over after the machines take the good work. They are, on reflection, the most important things humans do. Trust holds relationships and institutions together; judgment decides what is worth doing; meaning is what makes any of it matter. That the durable human core turns out to coincide with what is most deeply human is not an accident, and it suggests the AI era may push work toward, rather than away from, the things that were always most valuable.

Trust and Meaning

People want to be understood, trusted, and guided by other people, and that want does not diminish as machines grow more capable. If anything it intensifies. As outputs become abundant and nearly free, the scarce and valuable thing becomes the human relationship around them: the trust that a person has one's interests at heart, the meaning found in being genuinely understood. A great deal of real value has always lived in this relationship, and as the surrounding tasks are automated, that value becomes a larger share of the whole.

This has always been quietly true and is becoming obvious. The professional whose clients stay for decades, the manager whose team would follow them anywhere, the adviser whose word is trusted without question: their value was never mainly in the tasks they performed, which could often have been done by someone else. It was in the relationship, and relationships are built by humans, for humans, in ways no model can manufacture. The automation of tasks simply reveals where the value always lived.

Judgment and Wisdom

In an age of abundant answers, the scarce thing is good judgment about which answers matter. Knowing what to do, what is worth doing, and what is right requires context, values, and hard-won experience that resist automation, because they depend on understanding a particular situation in its full human richness. AI can generate options endlessly; deciding wisely among them, with an eye to consequences and values, remains a human act. Wisdom, the capacity to judge well in complex and novel situations, may be the least automatable capability of all.

This is why the people who thrive are rarely those with the most technical knowledge of the tools, which dates quickly, but those with the soundest judgment about how to use them. The tool can draft the contract, model the scenario, or generate the design; a person must still decide whether it is right, whether it is wise, and whether it serves the actual goal. As the generating becomes nearly free, the deciding becomes the scarce and valuable act, and judgment, the capacity to decide well, becomes the centre of a career rather than its periphery.

None of this means the tools are unimportant; a person who refuses to use them is not exercising judgment but neglecting it. The point is one of emphasis. Tool skill is necessary but no longer sufficient or scarce, while judgment about how and when to apply that skill is both scarce and rising in value. The durable strategy pairs genuine fluency with the tools, so that they can be used well, with the deeper human judgment that decides what is worth using them for.

Doubling Down on the Human

The strategy that follows is not to flee the technology but to use it deliberately for what it does, and to reinvest the freed capacity into the human core. The hours that AI reclaims from routine work are precisely the hours that can be poured into deepening judgment, building trust, and exercising creativity. The human advantage is not a fixed possession to be guarded but a set of capabilities to be cultivated, and the person who cultivates them while letting AI handle the rest holds an advantage that compounds rather than erodes.

Cultivating the human core is itself a kind of reinvention, run through the same loop. A person can audit where their judgment is weak, climb by deliberately seeking harder decisions, and build the trust and relationships that compound over years. None of this happens automatically with age; wisdom is earned by reflecting on experience, not merely accumulating it. The human advantage, in other words, is not a birthright that protects the idle but a capacity that rewards the person who keeps deepening it.

There is a reassurance in this for those who fear that experience has been devalued. The very capabilities that take years to build, judgment, wisdom, and a network of trust, are the ones that endure, while the purely technical skills that can be acquired quickly are the ones most exposed. Experience is not obsolete in the AI era; in the capabilities that matter most, it is more valuable than ever, provided it is paired with a willingness to keep learning the tools.

This durable core is what leadership rests on, and what makes a person valuable across every wave of change. Which raises the last and largest point of the book: that the waves do not stop, and the loop, therefore, never does either.

IN PRACTICE

A financial adviser watched AI tools begin to do much of what had once filled his days: building portfolios, running projections, generating reports. For a while it felt like a threat to everything he offered. Then his clients taught him otherwise.

What they valued, it turned out, was never the spreadsheet. It was the trust built over years, the judgment to know which goals truly mattered to a particular family, the steadiness in a frightening market, and the meaning he helped them find in their choices about money. The tools made the analysis cheap, and in doing so they made the human relationship the whole of his value rather than a part of it. He leaned into exactly what the machines could not do, the trust, the judgment, the empathy, and found his work more valuable, and more human, than before.

IN SHORT

- Competing with AI at speed, scale, and recall is a losing game; the human advantage lies in what AI structurally cannot do.
- The durable human core includes meaning, trust, ethics, judgment, empathy, creativity, and wisdom.
- These endure because they are unpredictable, non-automatable, and tacit: they cannot be forecast, reduced to rules, or fully written down.
- As outputs become cheap and abundant, human trust, judgment, and meaning become more valuable, not less.
- The strategy is to use AI for what it does and reinvest the freed capacity into deepening the human core.

ASK YOURSELF

1. Which parts of current value depend on the durable human core rather than on tasks AI can do?
2. Of meaning, trust, ethics, judgment, empathy, creativity, and wisdom, which are the real strengths?
3. Where is energy being wasted competing with AI on its own terms rather than on human ones?
4. What freed capacity could be reinvested into deepening the human core?

CHAPTER THIRTY-EIGHT

Reinvention Never Ends

It would be satisfying to end with the promise that running the loop once delivers a person to safety for good. It does not, and pretending otherwise would be the book's only dishonesty. The truth is more demanding and, in its way, more freeing: reinvention does not end, because disruption does not end. There is no final, safe version of a career to arrive at, only a way of working that keeps producing safety as the ground keeps moving.

This sounds, at first, like bad news, and for the person hoping to do the work once and be done it is. But the alternative on offer was never permanence; it was only the illusion of it. Careers that felt stable for decades were stable because change happened to be slow, not because they were immune to it. What has changed is the pace, not the principle, and the honest response is not to mourn a stability that was always conditional but to build the one capacity that does not depend on the world holding still.

There Is No Finish Line

AI itself will keep changing, in ways no one can fully predict, and beyond AI will come other shifts not yet named. Any plan built on the assumption that this is the last disruption is a plan built on sand. The discomfort of accepting this is real, but it is far smaller than the discomfort of being repeatedly surprised by a future that one had insisted would hold still. Accepting that change is permanent is the first step toward ceasing to be afraid of it.

History offers some comfort here, even as it removes the hope of a final rest. Every previous wave of technological change felt, to those living through it, like the end of the world of work, and each time the people who adapted found new ground on the other side. AI is genuinely different in important ways, but the deeper pattern holds: those who treat change as permanent and prepare for it fare far better than those who keep waiting for things to settle down. Things do not settle down; the skill is to stop needing them to.

Disruption Comes in Waves

Disruption is best pictured not as a single event but as a series of waves, each one met by another turn of the loop.

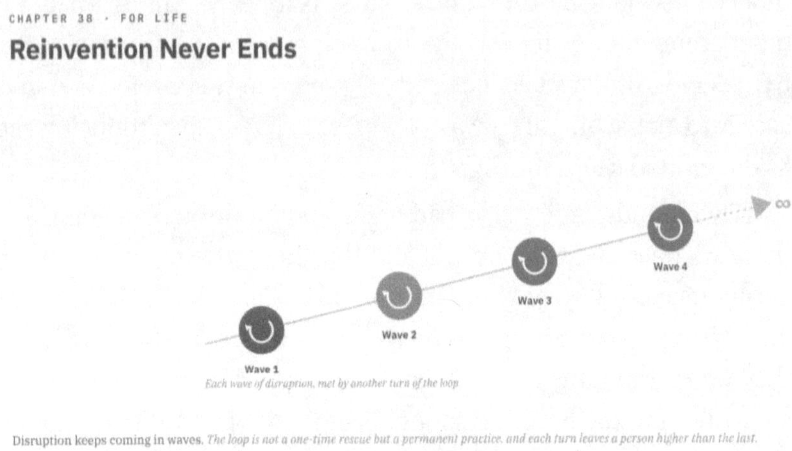

Figure 38.1 *Reinvention never ends: each wave of disruption is met by another turn of the loop, leaving a person higher than before.*

The crucial detail is that the waves do not simply repeat in place. Each turn of the loop leaves a person higher than the last, with more skill, a wider network, deeper confidence, and greater optionality, so that the next wave is met from a stronger position than the one before. The waves are perpetual, but so is the compounding, and the compounding favours whoever keeps running the loop through every one of them.

The compounding is what turns a frightening prospect into an encouraging one. A person standing at the first wave, with no new skills, no wider network, and no confidence in their ability to adapt, faces it at its most threatening. The same person at the fifth wave, having met four already, faces it with a deep reserve of exactly the things that make adaptation easy. The waves may even grow larger, but the capacity to meet them grows faster, and that race is the one that decides whether a career thrives or merely survives.

This is why the early cycles deserve patience even when they feel unrewarding. The first turn of the loop is the hardest and the least immediately profitable, and it is tempting to conclude from it that the whole effort is not worth it. But the first cycle is buying the foundation that makes every later one easier, and judging the method by its first turn is like judging a long investment by its first month. The returns, in reinvention as in anything that compounds, come to those who stay in long enough to collect them.

The Loop Is for Life

Run a single time, the loop saves a job. Run for a lifetime, it becomes something larger: a permanent operating system for a career, a default way of working that quietly keeps a person current, useful, and valuable through whatever comes. This is the real prize the book has been pointing at. Not a one-time escape from a single disruption, but a durable capacity to meet any disruption, which is worth far more than safety from this particular one.

Seen this way, the question that opened the book, how to escape AI disruption, has a slightly different answer than it first appears. There is no single escape, no door a person walks through once into permanent safety. There is only a way of moving that keeps a person ahead of the disruption as it travels, the way a skilled sailor is never finished with the wind but is also never at its mercy. The loop is that way of moving, and the skill it builds is not escape from change but ease within it.

Why This Is Good News

Perpetual reinvention can sound exhausting, a treadmill that never stops. In practice it is the opposite, because once the loop becomes a habit, change stops being a threat. The fear that surrounds disruption comes from feeling unprepared for it; a person who reinvents by default is never unprepared. For them, the next wave is not a crisis but a familiar season, met with the calm of someone who has done this before and knows they can do it again. The habit that looks like effort is what buys the freedom from fear.

There is a kind of peace in this that is hard to reach any other way. The person who depends on the world not changing lives in quiet dread of the news that it has; the person who expects change and knows how to meet it is freed from that dread entirely. They can watch a new technology arrive with curiosity rather than alarm, because they have a reliable answer to the only question that matters, which is what they will do about it. That peace is not the absence of disruption but the presence of a method.

Stay Curious, Useful, Valuable

Three simple dispositions keep the loop running for life. The first is curiosity: a standing willingness to keep learning, which turns each new development into something interesting rather than threatening. The second is usefulness: a continual focus on solving real problems for real people, which is what makes a person worth keeping in any era. The third is visible value: the habit of ensuring the worth created is seen. Curious, useful, and valuable, sustained over a career, is the entire disposition a durable working life requires.

These three dispositions are also, not coincidentally, what makes a working life satisfying rather than merely secure. Curiosity makes the work interesting; usefulness makes it meaningful; visible value makes it respected. A career run on these terms is not a defensive crouch against a threatening future but an engaged, forward-leaning way of working that happens also to be durable. The method that protects a career, in the end, turns out to be much the same as the method that makes one worth having.

It is fitting that the book's practical advice and its deeper hope converge here. The reader who takes nothing else away might hold on to this: that the way to be safe in a changing world is not to find a place the change cannot reach, which does not exist, but to become the kind of person who meets change well, which anyone can. Curiosity, usefulness, and visible value are not only a survival strategy. They are a good way to work, and a good way to work is the most durable security there is.

The loop, run for life, is the method this book has tried to give. What remains is to say plainly what it all amounts to, and why running from AI was never the way to escape it. That is the work of the conclusion.

IN PRACTICE

A veteran photographer had reinvented herself more times than she could easily count. She had survived the collapse of film, the arrival of digital, the flood of smartphone cameras, and the rise of cheap stock libraries, each time by learning the new tools and finding the value that remained scarce. When AI image generation arrived, colleagues panicked; she recognized an old pattern.

She did what she had always done: tested the new tools, found what they could and could not do, and repositioned toward the work that still needed a human eye and a human relationship. It was not that she was fearless; it was that she had run the loop so many times that another wave felt less like a catastrophe and more like a familiar season. Decades of reinvention had taught her the one thing that truly lasts, which is not any particular skill but the capacity to keep acquiring new ones. The next wave, whatever it turned out to be, would find her ready.

IN SHORT

- There is no finish line; AI will keep changing, and other disruptions will follow, so no career is ever permanently safe.
- Disruption comes in waves, and the loop is the practice that meets each one, leaving a person higher than before.

- The loop is not a one-time rescue but a permanent operating system for a working life.
- Perpetual reinvention is freeing rather than exhausting: once it is a habit, change stops being a threat.
- Staying curious, useful, and valuable is the disposition that keeps the loop running for life.

ASK YOURSELF

1. Is the next wave of disruption being treated as a catastrophe or as a familiar season?
2. Is the loop currently a one-time effort, or is it becoming a permanent habit?
3. Which of curiosity, usefulness, and visible value most needs attention to keep the loop running?
4. What would it mean to be ready for a disruption that has not yet been named?

CONCLUSION

You Do Not Escape AI by Running From It

The title of this conclusion is also its argument. There is a powerful instinct, when faced with a force as large as AI, to run from it: to avoid the tools, to downplay the change, and to hope to reach the end of a career before it fully arrives. This book has argued, at length, that running does not work. The disruption is too broad and too fast to outrun, and the attempt to do so only guarantees being caught from a position of weakness rather than strength. The way out is not away from AI but through it.

This is not a comfortable message, and the book has tried not to pretend otherwise. Engaging with a technology that threatens one's livelihood is harder, in the short term, than ignoring it, and the loop demands real and continued effort. But the comfort of avoidance is borrowed against a future that arrives regardless, and the effort of engagement is the only version that leaves a person stronger rather than merely later to the reckoning. The choice the book has insisted on is the harder one precisely because it is the one that works.

None of this is a promise that the path is easy or that every story ends well; disruption is real, and it does real harm to real people, often unfairly. What the book offers is not a guarantee but the best available response: a method that improves the odds, shifts the balance from fear toward agency, and gives a person something to do other than wait and hope. In a situation no one chose, the ability to act well is itself a kind of freedom, and it is the freedom this book has tried to hand over.

Escape, in the sense this book has meant it, is not flight. It is transformation. A person who escapes AI disruption does not end up somewhere the technology cannot reach; they end up someone for whom it is an advantage rather than a threat. The path to becoming that person has filled these pages, but in the end it reduces to five moves.

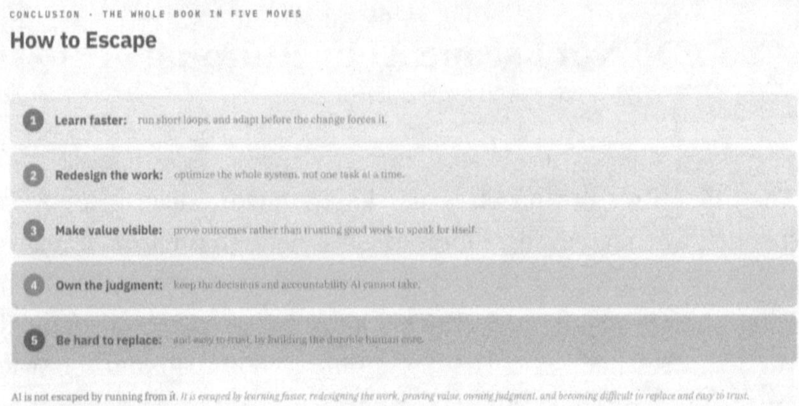

How to Escape *The whole book, reduced to five moves that turn AI from a threat into an advantage.*

Each of the five has filled chapters, yet together they are simple. Learning faster, through short loops, means adapting before the change forces it. Redesigning the work as a system means capturing the large gains that task-by-task tinkering always misses. Making value visible means the worth a person creates is seen by the people who decide. Owning the judgment means keeping the decisions and the accountability that AI cannot take. And becoming hard to replace and easy to trust means building the durable human core that no tool can copy.

These five moves are not a checklist to be completed once but a stance to be held continuously, and they are easier to hold together than apart, because each supports the others. Learning faster surfaces what to redesign; redesigning creates value worth making visible; visible value rests on judgment worth owning; and judgment, trust, and the human core are what finally make a person hard to replace. Run together, they are not five separate tasks but one coherent way of working.

What unites the five is a single shift in stance: from defending against AI to building with it. The person who runs from the technology spends their energy on a doomed rearguard action, fighting to preserve a way of working that the world has already left behind. The person who runs the loop spends the same energy becoming more capable, more visible, and more valuable, and arrives not merely safe but ahead. The fear that drives the running is real, but the running is exactly the wrong response to it.

It is worth saying plainly that this is within reach for ordinary people, not only for the technically gifted or the already secure. Nothing in the method requires genius, youth, or a particular field; it asks only for the willingness to look honestly at one's work, to learn steadily, and to keep going. The professionals whose stories fill these pages were not exceptional in their talents. They were exceptional only in their decision to engage rather than flee, and that decision is available to anyone.

The future this book describes is not one without disruption, because no such future exists. It is one in which disruption has lost its power to frighten, because a person has the method to meet it, again and again, for as long as it keeps coming. That is the real escape: not from AI, which is going nowhere, but from the fear of being left behind by it. The tools will keep changing. The loop, run for life, is how a person changes with them, and stays, through every wave, difficult to replace and easy to trust.

ESCAPE AI DISRUPTION

Appendices

Worksheets, Templates, and Trackers

Twelve practical tools for running the escape, from the first self-assessment to the full ninety-day plan.

APPENDIX A

AI Disruption Self-Assessment

A quick way to gauge two things at once: how exposed the work is to AI, and how ready the person is to meet it. Each statement is rated from 1 (strongly disagree) to 5 (strongly agree). The two totals locate a starting point on the map.

Part 1: Exposure

Higher scores mean more of the work sits in AI's path, and more urgency to act.

Statement	1 2 3 4 5
A large share of the work is routine and repeatable.	1 2 3 4 5
Much of the work is processing information rather than exercising judgment.	1 2 3 4 5
The outputs of the role are mostly digital: text, data, code, or images.	1 2 3 4 5
AI tools can already do parts of the work at acceptable quality.	1 2 3 4 5
The field is changing quickly because of AI.	1 2 3 4 5
Few daily tasks depend on in-person human relationships.	1 2 3 4 5
Exposure total (6 to 30)	

Part 2: Readiness

Higher scores mean better preparation, and a stronger position from which to act.

Statement	1 2 3 4 5
The core AI tools for the field are already in regular use.	1 2 3 4 5
There is a steady habit of learning new tools and methods.	1 2 3 4 5
Time is protected each week for building skills.	1 2 3 4 5
The value created at work is visible to the people who decide.	1 2 3 4 5
The work draws on judgment, trust, or creativity that AI cannot easily copy.	1 2 3 4 5
There is a clear plan for adapting as AI advances.	1 2 3 4 5
Readiness total (6 to 30)	

Reading the result

- High exposure, low readiness: the most urgent quadrant. Begin the loop now, starting with the audit in Appendix E.
- High exposure, high readiness: well placed to lead. Move from adapting to leading adoption and coaching others.
- Low exposure, low readiness: time is on hand, but the habit is not. Build the reinvention board in Appendix G before the pressure arrives.
- Low exposure, high readiness: a strong position. Stay sharp, keep watching the boundary, and protect the lead.

APPENDIX B

The Human-AI Boundary Map (Worksheet)

List the real tasks of a typical week, then place each one on the line between human and machine work. The point is to map the work as it actually is, not as the job title suggests.

1. List every task that fills a typical week, in plain terms.
2. Place each task in one of the three zones below.
3. Mark the tasks where the boundary feels like it is moving.
4. Revisit the map every quarter; the line does not stay still.

Human core	Shared	AI-led
The human leads; AI stays out.	Human directs; AI drafts.	AI does; the human checks.

Remember: *the boundary keeps moving toward AI. A task in the human core today may be shared tomorrow, so the map is a snapshot, not a settlement.*

APPENDIX C

The Framework Toolkit: One-Page Reference Card

Every framework in the book, gathered in one place. The ESCAPE Loop is the spine; the rest are tools used at each turn of it.

The ESCAPE Loop

E	**Expose**	Audit the work honestly. See what AI can already do, and where the real exposure is.
S	**Shed**	Drop the low-value, repeatable work that AI does better. Stop defending it.
C	**Climb**	Move up to higher-value work: judgment, strategy, relationships, and originality.
A	**Augment**	Build human-AI workflows. Let AI amplify the work, and own the judgment.
P	**Prove**	Make the value visible: proof of work, case studies, and before-and-after results.
E	**Evolve**	Run a retro, adapt, and repeat. Reinvention is a loop, not a leap.

The supporting tools

Framework	In one line
The Delegation Test	Hand to AI what is repeatable, low in judgment, and easy to verify.
The OODA Loop	Observe, Orient, Decide, Act. AI speeds Observe; Orient and Decide stay human.
The AI Advantage Stack	Domain expertise, tool fluency, prompting, data interpretation, human influence, and storytelling, stacked together.

Framework	In one line
Levels of Oversight	In the loop (approve each step), on the loop (monitor), out of the loop (check after). Match the level to the stakes.
The Boundary Map	Place each task in the human core, the shared zone, or the AI-led zone.
The Reinvention Board	A simple Kanban for skills, experiments, and outcomes, run at a sustainable pace.
Time vs Assets	Trade hours for money, or build assets that earn beyond the hours. Aim for assets and optionality.
The Durable Human Core	Meaning, trust, ethics, judgment, empathy, creativity, and wisdom: valuable because they cannot be predicted, automated, or made explicit.
The 90-Day Roadmap	Set up, map exposure, build fluency, create value, and reinvent, across five phases.

APPENDIX D

30-Day AI Learning Tracker

The aim is simple: use AI tools on real work every day for thirty days. Fluency comes from repetition, not study, and a short daily note is enough to keep the habit honest and visible.

Goal: a daily AI habit, and one working AI-assisted workflow by day thirty.

Day	Tool / focus	What was practiced	Win or note
1			
2			
3			
4			
5			
6			
7			
8			
9			
10			
11			
12			
13			
14			

Day	Tool / focus	What was practiced	Win or note
15			
16			
17			
18			
19			
20			
21			
22			
23			
24			
25			
26			
27			
28			
29			
30			

APPENDIX E

Career Risk Mapping Template

A structured audit of the real work. For each task, weigh how much time it takes, how exposed it is to AI, and how much value it creates for others. The pattern points to a clear action for each one.

1. List the tasks that make up the role, one per row.
2. Rate each on time spent, AI exposure, and value to others, as High, Medium, or Low.
3. Choose an action: defend, augment, or shed.

Task	Time	AI exposure	Value	Action

Task	Time	AI exposure	Value	Action

Reading the map

- High value, low AI exposure: core work. Defend it and climb further into it.
- High value, high AI exposure: augment. Do it with AI, and own the judgment.
- Low value, high AI exposure: shed. Hand it to the tools and reclaim the time.
- Low value, low AI exposure: question whether it needs doing at all.

APPENDIX F

Human-AI Workflow Canvas

A canvas for redesigning one process as a single human-AI team. The goal is not to automate the whole thing, but to assign each step to whoever does it best, and to own the judgment that holds it together.

The process to redesign

The outcome it should produce

Step-by-step design

Step	Human does	AI does

Before and after

Before	After
Cycle time:	**Cycle time:**

Before	After
Quality / consistency:	**Quality / consistency:**

APPENDIX G

The Personal Reinvention Board (Kanban Template)

A board makes the invisible work of reinvention visible. Set a vision, fill a backlog, keep one small sprint active, and move cards to done. Run it at a sustainable pace, with a standing weekly retro.

Vision (one line: the person worth becoming)

Backlog	This sprint	Done

Cadence (hours per week):	Retro ritual (day and time):

Tag each card: a Skill to learn, an Experiment to run, or an Outcome to produce. Keep only a few cards in the active sprint at once.

APPENDIX H

Systems Map Worksheet: Find Your Leverage Points

Most work is a system, not a list of tasks. Mapping the system, its inputs, steps, outputs, and bottlenecks, reveals the leverage points where a small change produces an outsized gain.

The system being mapped (a role, a process, or a workflow)

Map the flow

Inputs	Steps	Outputs

Find the leverage

Where does the work slow down or pile up? (the bottlenecks)

Where would a small change create a large gain? (the leverage points)

Which step is the best candidate for an AI-assisted redesign?

APPENDIX I

Personal Retro and Sprint Template

The habit that keeps the loop improving. At the end of each cycle, run a short retro, then plan the next sprint. Honesty about what did not work is where most of the value is.

The retro

What worked	What did not	What to change

The next sprint

Goal for the coming sprint (one sentence)

The one to three cards to pull into the sprint

Hours committed, and when they are protected

APPENDIX J

Personal Reinvention Scorecard

A way to see progress over time. Rate each dimension from 1 (just starting) to 5 (strong), once a month for three months. The trend matters more than any single score.

Dimension	Month 1	Month 2	Month 3
Tool fluency: comfort using AI on real work			
Workflows: real tasks redesigned with AI			
Value shipped: proof of work and case studies			
Visibility: the value is seen by decision-makers			
Human core: judgment, trust, and creativity deepening			
Optionality: assets and paths beyond a single role			
Cadence: the loop is running at a steady pace			
Total (out of 35)			

Read the trend: a rising total means the loop is working. A flat total is a signal to revisit the cadence and the retro, not the ambition.

APPENDIX K

AI Tools Starter List

Specific tools change month to month, so this list is organized by category rather than by brand. The aim is to pick two or three that touch the highest-value parts of the work, and to reach fluency with those before adding more.

Category	What it does	Start here when
General assistant	A conversational model for drafting, summarizing, analysis, and asking questions.	The everyday starting point for most work.
Writing and editing	Drafting, rewriting, tightening, and adapting tone for an audience.	Useful in almost every knowledge role.
Research and search	Finding, gathering, and synthesizing information with sources.	When the work involves learning quickly.
Coding and analysis	Writing, explaining, and debugging code; working through data.	For technical and data-heavy roles.
Images and design	Generating and editing visuals, mockups, and diagrams.	For visual and creative work.
Audio and meetings	Transcribing, summarizing, and capturing actions from calls.	When meetings and notes consume time.
Automation	Connecting steps and tools so routine workflows run themselves.	Once a repeatable workflow is clear.

A note on choosing: the best tool is the one that fits the real work, not the one most talked about. Fluency with a few beats dabbling in many.

APPENDIX L

90-Day Escape Plan Workbook

The whole plan in one fillable place. Work through it in order, a phase at a time. It draws on the earlier appendices, so keep them to hand.

Day 0: Set up the board

Vision (one line)

First three backlog items

Weekly cadence, and the retro day

Days 1 to 15: Map exposure

☐ Listed the real tasks of a typical week.

☐ Placed each task on the Boundary Map (Appendix B).

☐ Tested AI against real work, rather than guessing.

Weak signals noticed (where the boundary is moving)

Days 16 to 30: Build fluency

The two or three core tools chosen

☐ Built a daily AI habit on real work.

☐ Practised prompting and problem framing.

☐ Shipped one working AI-assisted workflow.

Days 31 to 60: Create value

The one process being improved

Before (cycle time and quality) / After (cycle time and quality)

☐ Wrote up a before-and-after case study, with numbers.

Days 61 to 90: Reinvent

☐ Gathered proof of work into a small portfolio.

☐ Sharpened the value into a new offer, and stated it.

☐ Ran the first ninety-day retro (Appendix I).

The new offer, in one sentence

What the next ninety-day loop will change

---

www.ingramcontent.com/pod-product-compliance
Lightning Source LLC
LaVergne TN
LVHW100302210926
848480LV00003B/994